Amber Guyger and the Murder of Botham Jean

Ruth Cowens

Published by Trellis Publishing, 2021.

While every precaution has been taken in the preparation of this book, the publisher assumes no responsibility for errors or omissions, or for damages resulting from the use of the information contained herein.

AMBER GUYGER AND THE MURDER OF BOTHAM JEAN

First edition. July 1, 2021.

Copyright © 2021 Ruth Cowens.

ISBN: 979-8224856992

Written by Ruth Cowens.

AMBER GUYGER & THE MURDER OF BOTHAM JEAN

RUTH COWENS

<u>TRACEY GRISSOM</u>
<u>TED BUNDY</u>
<u>THE TRAILSIDE KILLER</u>
<u>TOY BOX KILLER</u>

Amber Guyger
September 6, 2018
At 9:59 p.m., a call came in to the Dallas 911 dispatch center.

(Phone ringing)

Caller: Get up man

Operator: Dallas 911. This is Carla. What is your emergency?

Caller: Hi this is an off-duty officer...

Um... can I get... I need EMS...

I'm in number..

Operator: What's your address?

Caller: Hold on...

Operator: Do you need police as well or just EMS?

Caller: Yes. I need both.

Operator: Okay what's your address?

Caller: F**k

I'm at apartment number 1478...

I'm in 1478.

Operator: And what's the address there?

Caller: Um, it's 1210 South Lamar.

1478... yes.

Operator: What's going on?

Caller: I'm an off-duty officer... I thought I was in my apartment. And I shot a guy thinking that he was... Thinking it was my apartment.

Operator: You shot someone?

Caller: Yes, I thought it was my apartment.

I'm f**ked.

Oh my god.

I'm sorry.

Operator: Okay and where are you at right now?

Caller: I'm in... What do you mean?

I'm inside the apartment with him...

Hey... come on man...

Operator: What's your name?

Caller: I'm Amber Guyger.

I need... get me... I'm...

I'm in...

Operator: Okay we have help on the way.

Amber: I know but I'm...

I'm gonna lose my job...

I thought it was my apartment.

Hey man.

Operator: (inaudible)

Amber: F**k

Operator: Okay, stay with me, okay?

Amber: I am. I am.

I need...

I know I need a supervisor.

Hey bud... Hey bud... Hey bud.

Come on.

I thought it was my apartment.

Operator: I understand. We have help on the way, okay?

Amber: I thought it was my apartment.

Hurry please...

Operator: They are on their way.

Amber: I need... I...

I thought it was my apartment. I thought it was my apartment.

I could have sworn I parked on the third floor.

Operator: Okay I understand.

Amber: No.

(Heavy breathing)

I thought it was my apartment. I thought it was my apartment. It was my apartment.

I thought it was my apartment.

Operator: What's the gate code there?

Amber: I don't know. I don't know.

Operator: You don't know? Okay.

Amber: I thought it was my apartment.

Operator: They're trying to get in there.

We have an officer there. You don't know the gate code?

Amber: No.

I thought it was my apartment.

I thought it was my apartment.

Operator: Okay and what floor are you in right now?

Amber: On the fourth floor. Fourth...

Hey bud, hey bud. They're coming they're coming...

I'm sorry man...

Operator: Okay, where was he shot?

Amber: He's on the top... top left.

(Silence...)

Operator: Okay, you're with Dallas PD, right?

Amber: Yes.

(Silence...)

Amber: Oh my god. I'm done.

I didn't mean to... I didn't mean to... I didn't mean to... I'm so sorry...

Hey bud...

Operator: They're trying to get there to you, okay?

Amber: I know...

Stay with me bud...

(Silence...)

Holy sh*t

Operator: Okay they're almost there... They're already there, they tried to get to you.

Amber: **** I thought it was my apartment. I thought it was my apartment.

Holy f**k. I thought it was my apartment... Oh my God...
****

I thought it was my apartment... I'm so sorry. I'm so sorry.
****

Oh my God.

Operator: Okay they're trying to get there to you. Do you hear them? Do you see them?

Amber: No. No... I... I...

How the f**k did I put the... How did I...

I'm so tired. Hurry.

Hey! Over here, over here!

Operator: Okay, go ahead and talk to them.

Amber: No, it's me! I'm off-duty! I'm off duty. I ****

I thought they were in my apartment... I thought this was my floor.

(Line goes dead)

Amber Guyger, a police officer at the Dallas Police Department, had just returned from a long shift at work, and as she had done countless times, opened her door. On the other side of the door was a black man in his underwear, and Amber realized that there was an intruder in the house. She directed him to put his hands up and when he failed to do so, she shot him. The intruder lay on the floor bleeding, seriously wounded. Amber then realized her mistake. She was not in her own apartment.

Lying on the floor of his own home was 26-year-old Botham Shem Jean. Paramedics got to the scene and quickly attended to Jean, who at the time was bleeding profusely from his chest wound. He was rushed to the Baylor University Medical Center where he was later pronounced dead. This was the night that started a year-long fight between the Dallas Police Department, the Rangers, Jean's family, and the community.

The Dallas County district attorney's office public integrity division response team was quickly called onto the scene. Since Guyger was a police officer, the team had to carry out its independent investigation. Guyger's blood was drawn and sent off to the lab for analysis.

The First 48 Hours

Amber Guyger's case did not follow the usual investigative protocol. On the night of, she was released and allowed to go home, and no charges were filed against her for shooting an unarmed man. This led to the community rallying behind the Jean family, as they speculated that Amber was receiving preferential treatment because she was a police officer. The news of Botham's death spread fast, and civil rights groups started gearing up to face the police department and to ensure that the case would not be swept under the rug, and that due diligence was done.

Allison Jean, Botham's mother, was in New York on the night of her son's tragic death. She was visiting Allisa Findley, Botham's

37-year-old sister. Allison had just said a prayer for her children, and lay down to sleep, and had no idea what was coming to disrupt her slumber. Allisa's phone rang just after her mother had gone to sleep. On the other side of the call was a social worker at the Baylor University Medical Center, and she had some chilling news. She explained that Botham had passed away in the hospital after he took a shot to the heart. The social worker had very little detail to add, and the conversation quickly came to an end. Alissa went to wake her mother up, and was trembling when Allison opened her eyes.

Allison Jean flew to Dallas to find out what happened to her son. She was received by sympathetic members of the community who, while they did not understand the pain she was going through, were angered by the injustice of it all. Amber Guyger was still free, and her son was lying on a cold slab in the coroner's office.

On Friday 7th September, Dallas Police Chief U. Renee Hall took to the stage to update the public on the developments pertaining to the events of the previous night. She stated that the Dallas Police Department would no longer be handling the case of the officer involved shooting, and that for transparency reasons, she had handed over the case to the Texas Rangers. The Rangers' investigation would be independent, and therefore there would be no favoritism or instances of misconduct. She stated that the officer had been placed on administrative leave, pending investigation. However, she admitted that the officer had not yet been interviewed by police, but that a search warrant had been obtained for Botham's home. According to the warrant, the officer had stated that she had gone to her apartment and was confronted by a man she thought was an intruder. Botham's neighbor stated that he heard voices, immediately followed by two gun shots. One of the shots had gone through the wall of Botham's apartment. The warrant had a list of items that were seized during the search, but the details were not released.

Chief Hall's press conference did little to placate the community. Amber Guyger was still free, and her actions drew more questions than answers. The hashtag #JusticeforBotham was taken up by the community as more people rallied behind the Jean family seeking answers. On 8th September, Texas Rangers officially took up the investigation, and the Dallas Police stepped down. Chief Hall issued another statement. This time, she stated that the warrant had not yet been signed by a judge because new information had been uncovered by the Rangers during their interview with the officer. She did not disclose what the new information was. At 8 p.m., the police finally released Guyger's name to the public. While the community had already figured out who the "officer in question" was, there had been no official statement confirming her identity.

Manslaughter Charge

After two days of calling out for justice for Botham and for the arrest of Amber Guyger, the family finally got their wish partially fulfilled. The Rangers issued a warrant for Guyger's arrest in relation to the death of Botham Shem Jean. On September 9th, Guyger turned herself in to the Kauffman County authorities. The county jail logs showed that she was booked at 7:20 p.m., but did not stay at the facility for long. She quickly posted the $300,000 bail and was released within an hour.

There was little to celebrate about after Guyger's arrest. The Jean family found out that Guyger had been indicted on a manslaughter charge, and the community was outraged. Ministers and community members started calling for the police to change the charge to a murder indictment since Botham was unarmed and in his own home. This charge sparked the racial debate, and the department was accused of being easy on Guyger because she was white and her victim was black. The protests grew, and the case quickly gained the attention of the nation.

That same day, even though their investigation was incomplete, the Rangers turned over the case to the Dallas County district attorney's office. However, they still maintained that the investigation was not yet closed.

Amber's Official Statement

September 10th was a turning point for the family of Botham Jean. Texas Rangers finally released the affidavit pertaining to the arrest warrant issued against Amber Guyger. In it were details about Guyger's official statement to the police. The 30-year-old stated that on the night of the shooting, she had just come home, her apartment was at the South Side Flats in the Cedars, from a 15-hour shift and parked her car on her floor. She then walked to her door, and took out her unique door key. The key had a special chip embedded in it. She then put the key into the key-hole. According to the affidavit, the "respective interior floor plans are in most ways identical or extremely similar." The force of the key being inserted into the door pushed the door open, as it had been slightly ajar at the time. The apartment was dark, and Guyger saw a "large silhouette." She immediately thought she was being burglarized, and drew her weapon.

Guyger gave verbal commands to the figure, and when the individual did not comply, she shot twice. One of the bullets struck Botham in the torso, and the other one went through a wall in the apartment. Once the individual was down, Guyger then called 911 and began administering first aid. She then turned on the lights and went to the front door, and that was when she realized it was not her apartment.

Guyger's narrative seemed plausible, but many doubted her account. She claimed that the door was slightly ajar when she put the key in, but this was proven to be highly unlikely. A tenant in the same building posted a video showing that the doors had an automatic lock system. She opened the door and let it go, and the door slammed shut. This was only one of the issues raised regarding Guyger's statement.

Allison Jean stated that her son was not the type to leave his door unlocked, let alone open. Lee Merrit and Benjamin Crump, attorneys for the Jean family, held a news conference on WFAA-TV. Merrit stated that independent witnesses had come forward and that their narratives poked holes in Guyger's story. Two witnesses stated that they heard knocking before the gunshots rang out. One witness stated that he heard a woman say, "Let me in. Let me in," while another thought she heard a man's voice say, "Oh my God, why did you do that." The second witness did not go to police with her story, but instead reached out to Botham's family to let them know that Guyger's story was not entirely accurate. However, no one could dispute Guyger's statement conclusively.

Search Warrants

The Rangers' search warrant for Botham's apartment included more information in addition to Guyger's statement. However, the information obtained from Guyger was later used to increase the scope of their search, and this led to a delay in the search. Guyger stated that the door was ajar, leading the Rangers to speculate that Botham may have been waiting for an unnamed visitor that night. This prompted them to add his phone and computer to the list of items that they wanted to seize for further analysis. According to sources close to the Jean family, Botham's laptop had been damaged on the night of, no one knows by whom, and it was never analyzed. No information about the phone was released by the Rangers, and it was unclear whether any pertinent information was ever recovered. However, the Rangers did release information that they found 10.4 grams of marijuana as well as a marijuana grinder in his home. This detail sparked anger in the community and particularly Botham's family. The department came under fire for trying to criminalize the victim, and the falimy's lawyer asked the police to explain what traces of marijuana had to do with Botham being killed in his own home. The Dallas police department and the Rangers did not offer any respond to the criticisms. Lee Merritt stated; "I think it is unfortunate that law enforcement begin to immediately criminalize the victim — in this case, someone who was clearly was the victim that has absolutely no bearing on the fact that he was shot in his home." Also recovered from the apartment were two fired cartridge casings, a ballistic vest with "police" markings, a laptop, and two used packages of medical aid.

A day after the Rangers released the affidavit, the Dallas County district attorney's office executed their search warrants. The warrants listed the electronic door locks from Guyger's and Botham's apartments as items that were to be seized. According to the Swiss manufacturer, Dormakaba, the locks on the doors at the South Side Flats stores data on 200 entries, and are unlocked by an RFID (Radio-Frequency Identification) chip. Dormakaba's website stated that the data stored included the time and date that a door is accessed, as well as the username or identification number of the person that accessed the door. The DA's office wanted to find out whether Guyger went to her home first before heading to Botham's apartment, or if Botham's door was unlocked from the inside, or ajar. The team also seized videos and photos from Botham's apartment and took laser measurements of the bullets' trajectory.

On 12th of September, the DA's office was granted another search warrant, this time for the complex's surveillance footage on the night of the shooting, and all the access and entry logs for the complex. No details were released pertaining to the DA's warrants.

Guyger's Termination and Grand Jury Hearing

By 13th of September, the Jean family was calling for the termination of Guyger's employment from the Dallas police department. The request was picked up by various civil rights' groups, who found it unfair the Guyger was only put on administrative leave for her actions. Chief Hall maintained that she was not authorized to terminate the employment of any employee in the police department. This did not sit right with a lot of people. Chief Hall's statement claimed that civil service laws prohibited her from firing Guyger. She did not state the specific law.

However, Chief Hall's decision not to terminate Guyger's employment was reversed on Monday, 24th of September. The Dallas Police Department released a statement titled: Chief U. Renee Hall Terminates Officer. It read:

> Dallas Police Chief U. Renee Hall terminated Police Officer Amber Guyger, #10702, during a hearing held September 24, 2018.

> An Internal Affairs investigation concluded that on September 9, 2018, Officer Guyger, #10702, engaged in adverse conduct when she was arrested for Manslaughter.

> Officer Guyger was terminated for her actions. She was hired in November 2013 and was assigned to the Southeast Patrol Division.

> Under civil service rules, Officer Guyger has the right to appeal her discipline.

On the same day, Botham's funeral was held in St. Lucia. He was buried in a cemetery by the sea.

In Dallas, a grand jury had been convened to decide the charges that Guyger would be facing in court. On Monday November 26th, the grand jury began its proceedings. The purpose was to determine whether Guyger would be charged with murder, manslaughter, or would face no charges. At the end of Monday's session, there was still more evidence to be presented, and the grand jury was re-convened on Wednesday 28th November. Botham's family was in Dallas in case they were called to give testimony, but were skeptical about the outcome of the grand jury. Protests were still in full swing, and activists were ready to take to the streets if Guyger was set free again. The grand jury proceedings were sealed, and no one except the prosecutors was privy to the evidence brought forward. However, the Jean family attorneys later confirmed that Allison Jean and Allysa Findley, Botham's mother and sister, did testify. After Wednesday's proceeding, the grand jurors left without voting on the charges to be brought against Guyger. They then re-convened on Friday and cast their votes. Guyger was indicted on a murder charge. The court documents revealed that the indictment was a "grand jury referral," meaning that the prosecutors sought for a murder count and not the original manslaughter charge that the Rangers had brought against Guyger.

Guyger, who had since moved out of the complex to unknown location, finally resurfaced at the Mesquite jail after the grand jury's indictment. She turned herself in at 1 p.m., and just like the previous time, was not held for long. She quickly posted the $200,000 bond and was free again.

Gag Order, Continuances, Trial, and Conviction

On January 8th 2019, Amber Guyger's first court date commenced. However, no proceedings took place in the courtroom. Guyger's attorneys, Robert Rogers and Toby Shook, met with the prosecutor, Jason Hermus, and State District Judge Tammy Kemp in the judge's chambers. Judge Kemp issued a gag order, effectively prohibiting the lawyers from speaking publicly about the case. According to sources, Guyger was not present during the meeting.

On March 18th, Guyger once again appeared in court for an announcement setting. While Guyger's presence wasn't mandatory, she was needed there in case Judge Kemp asked to see her. During the informal hearing, Guyger's trial date was set for August 12th. The prosecution presented the judge with a subpoena they needed her to sign, which she did. The subpoena was for records pertaining to any cruises Guyger took on Royal Caribbean between September 23 and March 4.

On April 1st, Guyger's lawyers filed a motion seeking for a continuance. They stated that Toby Shook, Guyger's lawyer, would be the lead attorney in another federal case that was going to trial at the end of July. For this reason, they felt that they wouldn't have enough time to provide Guyger with proper defense. Judge Kemp granted them the continuance, and Guyger's trial was moved from August 12th to September 23rd.

On Monday April 29th, Guyger's 911 call was released by WFAA-TV. Referring to the recording, Allison Jean said, "The call made me strengthen my view that Amber Guyger is a cold-blooded killer because she was more concerned about losing her job than my son, the value of my son. She does not sound like she was trying to help him at all." On Tuesday, Dallas police issued a statement saying that the department had opened an investigation into the release of Guyger's 911 recording. The Texas attorney general's office had ruled that the recording could be withheld by the department because of the pending criminal investigation, and the release of the recording had not been authorized by the department.

On July 8th, Guyger's lawyers are back in court. This time, they filed a motion seeking to move the trial out of Dallas, citing "media hysteria." They requested that the trial be moved to Collin, Grayson, Ellis, Rockwall, Kaufman, or Fannin County. They provided 297 articles that had been published about Botham's death as their evidence. They maintained that the media was spreading a false narrative "merely because ... [Guyger] is white and Mr. Jean was black, the incident must have been racial in nature." They concluded that the "publicity surrounding this case has been prejudicial and inflammatory." Two days later, the prosecution filed their counter-motion objecting to the defense's motion requesting a change in venue. They asked Judge Kemp to hold a hearing to consider the case's publicity, the evidence to be presented, and what the potential jurors would say during jury selection. They also requested that Judge Kemp hold off on ruling until the jurors were selected. On August 12th, Judge Kemp issued a court order stating that she would not rule on the matter until the process of questioning potential jurors was over or if it was apparent during the process "that a fair and impartial jury cannot be selected in Dallas County due the pervasive publicity in this case."

Jury selection started on September 6th, with hundreds of potential jurors present. On September 13th, Judge Kemp notified twelve jurors and four alternates that they have been selected. On 16th September, she denied the defense's motion to change the venue, and the case was set to be tried in Dallas.

On September 23rd, Guyger's trial finally started. Jurors were presented with various testimonies, including Amber Guyger's. She was the first witness the defense put on the stand, and she profusely apologized for her actions. Also presented was body cam footage of responding officers' trying to resuscitate Botham, and this was mistakenly shown while the Jean family was still in the courtroom. Judge Kemp quickly apologized for the oversight. By 28th September, the prosecution and defense had presented their evidence and witnesses, and were ready for closing arguments. On September 30th, the defense maintained that their client's "series of horrible events" led to the tragic death of Botham Jean. The jury began their deliberations after closing arguments, but had not yet come to a decision by 5 p.m. when they retired for the day. The jury was asked to consider "the castle doctrine" as well as the "sudden passion" defense. After a combined total of five hours of deliberation over two days, the jury finally returned a guilty verdict. Guyger maintained a calm demeanor after the verdict was read, but quickly sank into her chair after the jury left the courtroom.

The sentencing hearing was scheduled after a lunch recess on the same day. The Jean family testified during the sentencing hearing, with Brandt Jean, Botham's 18-year-old brother, hugging Guyger after his testimony. Guyger was sentenced to ten years in prison, with parole eligibility set at five years. After her sentencing, Judge Kemp stepped from her bench, gifted Guyger a Bible and then proceeded to give her a hug. Kemp has since come under fire for her actions, with activists claiming she only did it because Guyger was a white ex-cop.

The Murder of Joshua Brown

On October 4th, three days after Guyger was sentenced to 10 years in prison, a key witness in the case was gunned down a block from the apartment complex. Joshua Brown was a key witness for the prosecution, and testified that he heard voices shortly before Botham was shot. Many speculated that his death was connected to the case, but two suspects in custody have refuted this, claiming that Brown was shot because of a drug deal gone bad.

A KILLER SWEDISH GIRL

When a young Swedish woman named Annika Ostberg was incarcerated in the United States for participating in a double murder, her home country came to her defense. Even though they didn't have plenty of details on what really occurred in 1981, the citizens rallied together in order to get her released as soon as possible. She became a household name in her home country and a large number of the Swedish population saw her as someone who was wronged by the United States.

Annika had been arrested for her involvement in a robbery gone awry. She was with her drug dealing boyfriend Bob Cox during a crime spree which left both a restauranteur and a sheriff deputy dead. But did Annika pull the trigger or was she an innocent bystander?

Early life

Annika Östberg was born as Annika Maria Östberg on January 6th, 1954 in Stockholm, Sweden. She lived with her mother in Hässelby, a comfortable neighborhood in Stockholm. They had a very comfortable life up until the point when Annika's father decided to leave them. He mother quickly fell in love with another man, but he was an American citizen. He invited Annika's mother to come live with him in the USA and she agreed. Annika was only ten years old and she didn't want to leave Sweden. They would come to San Francisco in 1964, going from a conservative Swedish neighborhood to the free-wheeling drug culture of the growing San Francisco hippie movement.

Annika's dissatisfaction with the move manifested through a very strained relationship she had with her step-father. He was a wealthy businessman who wanted to provide both for his new wife and her daughter. But Annika would later claim that he was very distant and didn't show any emotions towards her. She blamed him for the move and refused to do any work at home or at school. Annika was bullied by her peers because she didn't speak English and couldn't learn the language no matter how much she tried. The problems kept piling up and eventually, Annika left her home when she was only thirteen. A runaway on the streets, she got involved with a sketchy crowd that used drugs and committed petty crimes. Annika claimed she began using drugs to fit in, becoming a full-fledged heroin addict by fourteen.

Promiscuous sex followed. Annika would become pregnant at the age of sixteen. Her conscience getting to her, Annika wanted to get clean for her baby. She cried and sweated her way through the process, managing to kick the heroin habit before the baby would come. She decided to have the baby at home without any medical assistance as she knew the hospital personnel would see the needle marks on her arms and alert Child Protective Services.

She had a baby with a man named "Greene Johnson" but he was of no help. Annika turned to prostitution and stripping to provide for the young child whom she named Sven. She would man a man named Brian Deasy who wanted to help Annika change her life. The two would move to Stockton, CA where they would marry. Things were fine for a few months as Annika adjusted to becoming a housewife. The lure of the drugs would prove to be too much, however, and she began jonesing for a hit. She abandoned the child and moved back to the lurid streets of San Francisco, resuming her life as a drug addicted prostitute.

Brushes with the law

Annika's San Francisco apartment became central headquarters for druggies and other sketchy characters. It wasn't unusual to find at least a couple of people sleeping on the floor, or casually hanging out. In 1972, a young man named Donald McKay was found dead in her apartment. After short questioning, Annika did admit that she planned to kill McKay. Other people who were present in the apartment at the time told the police that Annika's then-boyfriend murdered the man, but the law enforcement focused on her. Annika was already under investigation by the police, so they arrested her, and the judge gave her five years probation because the case itself lacked physical evidence or witnesses who were willing provide the proof that Annika killed McKay in her apartment.

Undaunted by beating a murder rap, Annika turned to theft. She would be caught stealing later that year and the judge was lenient, giving her eighteen months of probation. but Annika could not stay out of trouble. A few months later, she would be charged with possession of illegal substances. The judge then extended the sentence to three years probation during which she was supposed to get off drugs. Amazingly, she stayed out of trouble with the law for the three years only to find herself back in trouble a few weeks after her probation period expired. She was arrested for buying liquor for a minor which led to spending one day behind bars, as well as another twelve months of probation time.

Refusing to contact her mother, stepfather, or her child, Annika was clearly spiraling out of control. Her own lifestyle was very dangerous because she got involved with one of the well-known drug dealers in the area named Bob Cox. Bob Cox was a seasoned criminal who served jail sentences all over the world, including Turkey. The two of them started their tumultuous relationship at the beginning of the 1980s and their mutual drug addictions became worse. The couple was soon penniless, so they started thinking about different ways how to get more money. Bob Cox was willing to rob a place without any hesitation, and Annika agreed to help.

The robbery and murder

It was April 30th, 1981 when the couple got into their truck with the intent to commit a robbery. Choosing a place to rob was very difficult for Annika and Bob. But they did think about it a lot and remembered Joe Torre who was a restaurant owner. Annika Östberg did plenty of illegal work that included selling stolen goods. She knew Torre because she made numerous deliveries to his restaurant. Torre was happy to pay her a lot of money for stolen meat because it was cheaper. The official vendors were too expensive for him. The desperate couple saw Torre as low hanging fruit.

Torre's warehouse was in the northern part of San Francisco. Annika and Bob got into the truck which was filled with empty boxes to serve as a cover-up. The plan was that Bob would hide in the back and Torre would let Annika in with the truck, suspecting nothing. Once Annika rang the door on the warehouse, Torre opened, letting the vehicle pass the gate. Annika went to the back, pretending to unload the goods, and opened the door for Bob to come out and shoot Torre. The couple ransacked the warehouse and gathered up anything of value they could find. They were ready to get out of the city so they headed north to the Lake County. The reason for this was the fact that Östberg's son lived there with his father. She wanted to see the boy once again before going into hiding.

With the crime in San Francisco still undiscovered, the couple's vehicle broke down in the middle of the road. That was completely unplanned, and they were not prepared for this scenario. Sgt. Helbush who was on a patrol in the area saw the truck and asked if the couple needed help. According to Annika, Bob Cox shot Sgt. Helbush in the head while she was searching for her driver's license because she was behind the wheel. Once the man was on the ground, Cox shot him several more times. On the other hand, forensic experts argue that there was a little bit of evidence which could prove that Annika shot Sgt.

Helbush herself as he was walking back to his patrol car. He had a total of three bullet wounds in his back, and one in his head.

Knowing that they murdered a police officer, the couple dragged his body to the side of the road. They stole the officer's wallet, service pistol and police car. Back at Lake County Police Station, the dispatcher tried to contact Sgt. Helbush but got no answer. Suspecting that something might have happened to the man, they sent out another patrol car to search for him. His typical route was planned ahead, and they knew he was heading from Clearlake to Lakeport. His shift was ending. Soon enough, the police officer spotted Sgt. Helbush's body on the side of the road. His car was gone, so they presumed that the killer stole the vehicle.

The entire Lake County Police Station was alerted about the car and were warned that a killer possibly stole it. They started combing the area, looking for any trace of the vehicle. Don Anderson, who was Lake County Sheriff's deputy at that time saw the car near the base of Cobb Mountain. He immediately changed his direction and started chasing the stolen vehicle. Deputy Anderson informed other patrol cars in the area about what was happening, and they were all heading there to try to catch the killer. Cox was driving the car and he started panicking when he noticed that a police car was behind them. The road itself was not well kept, so driving on it wasn't easy. Cox hit a sharp turn and crashed. Both Annika and Cox were unharmed and conscious, so they got out of the car and tried to flee on foot. But they didn't get too far because Deputy Anderson was right there behind them. He started shooting at the couple, so they fired back, hiding near the car wreckage.

Deputy Anderson managed to shoot Cox a couple of times and knowing that he might die, the killer surrendered. Deputy Anderson sustained a leg wound during the shooting, but it was not serious. Annika, on the other hand, claimed that she didn't shoot at the officer but only helped Cox reload the gun. After Cox reached the deputy officer with his hands up in the air, Annika was still hiding. Anderson approached her, and she agreed to surrender. However, as he tried to put the cuffs on her, Annika jumped and attempted to reach the gun which was laying on the ground. He was holding Cox with one hand while grabbing Annika with the other. Other officers arrived at the scene during this time, immediately pulling their guns on Annika. Deputy Anderson would become a local hero because he singlehandedly caught both criminals.

The suicide

After the arrest, Cox and Östberg were transported and detained in Lake County Jail in LakeportHowever, Cox took his own life in a jail cell before he even got in front of a judge. He used sheets from his bed in order to hang himself. Cox knew that he was facing a death penalty and he simply couldn't go through with it. The police suspected that Östberg might try to harm herself as well, so she was put on suicide watch.

"They made a suicide pact that only he was serious about," Deputy Anderson said. Sometime after Cox's suicide, the prosecution decided to move forward with the case. Annika was aware of her potential sentencing, and she appeared in front of a judge once again to explain that she was under the influence of drugs and that her mind was very cloudy. She was going for sympathy in order to receive a lighter sentence. The judge ordered a blood test, and it came back negative. She had been clean for over two months.

The trial

The trial started in 1982, and Annika's defense relied heavily on her history of drug use. They presented her as a victim who went through a tough childhood and even tougher adolescence. Her awyers didn't sugarcoat her past and they confirmed that their client had a long history of offenses. However, they also claimed that her lifestyle was to blame. After all, she wouldn't have met Cox if she wasn't a drug addict. When Annika took the stand, she repeated her story of the drug use during the time of the murder and that she was simply following Cox's lead. After all, she wasn't an active participant in either murder. Annika emphasized the fact that she was a witness to the crimes and not a participant.

The prosecution painted a different picture, starting off the case with the blood test which confirmed that Annika wasn't on drugs when the murders were committed. They also presented circumstantial evidence that she was responsible for the murder of Sgt. Helbush. Annika denied that she had anything to do with it and that Cox surprised her with the decision to shoot the officer. While it was easy to put the blame on the man who couldn't defend himself or tell his version of the events, it seemed like some of the people who were present in the courtroom believed in these claims.

The trial lasted months. All of the witnesses gave their testimonies, and now it was time to determine Annika's fate. Inexplicably, Annika stopped the procedures by taking a plea deal while the court already decided that they couldn't give her a death penalty because they had no proof that she actually killed anyone. She received a penalty of 25 years in prison to life.

There was something that gave Annika hope that she might get released eventually. She spoke to her lawyers after the trial, and they told her that the sentencing itself was better than they imagined. After all, there was a possibility that she could get paroled after serving twelve and a half years. This was a standard practice back in the 1980s and prisoners who behaved well during their incarceration could be released sooner. But the justice system did see many reforms during the time Annika spent in prison and new regulations were added.

Life in prison

Annika already served two and a half years when she received her sentence. She was held in a maximum security prison and spent her days on the death row during the trial. After all, the majority of people expected that she will end up there in the end. Life on death row was incredibly tough for Annika, but she found solace in writing. It was something she had never done before, and it filled out the empty hours she had in front of her. Writing served as Annika's therapy and it helped her grow as a person.

She continued to write even after her move from the death row. But finding writing supplies was a lot easier now. Annika's first book was released in 1999 while she was still in prison. It was co-written with Lena Katarina Swanberg and it told the story of Annika's life. Astonishingly, the book became a best seller in her native Sweden. Annika would later publish two more books, both of them dealing with her time behind the bars and the struggles that come with it.

Reactions in Sweden

Annika had became a celebrity of sorts in Sweden during her trial. The Swedish media wrote extensively about the case, with several long articles published each week. The trial was followed by everyone because Annika Östberg was from that country and people wanted to know what will happen to her. Even though the journalists had little information to go on, they reported on everything related to the case. It was almost impossible to get any confirmed statements from the police in California, so the journalists started communicating with Annika's relatives who told them what they knew.

According to them, Annika was not armed, and she followed her boyfriend's lead. It was almost unthinkable to them that someone could be sentenced to a life in prison even though they didn't actually commit a murder or harm anyone. Since her boyfriend was gone, the public in Sweden came to the conclusion that the United States jurisdiction system needed to find someone to blame for the killings. One of their police officers was a victim, and they felt the urge to lock up the easiest target, regardless of the level of their involvement. Annika was by Cox's side, so she was the perfect scapegoat.

The justice system in Northern Europe is completely different from the one they have in the United States. If a similar crime is committed in Sweden, the accused would get a really short sentence. She would probably spend up to seven years in prison if the murders happened over there, and released afterward. Therefore, the sentencing itself was incredibly strange to the citizens of Sweden. The outrage was instant and a couple of petitions were started immediately. The officials were trying to get Annika Östberg back to Sweden in order to serve her sentence in one of their prisons.

Of course, there were others who thought that Annika was guilty of the murders and that the obsession with bringing her back to her home country was not a good move. As the information kept reaching Sweden, they received more and more details about the crimes. But the damage was already done, and the majority of the public believed in the first version of the events. The critics accused the Swedish officials of being one-sided because Annika was from Sweden, and that was the only reason why they wanted her back.

Return to Sweden and the release

Annika Östberg's pleas to return to Sweden were rejected four times, the first one being in 1997. But things started moving forward in the spring of 2009 when California Board of Parole Hearings reviewed her case once again. Annika stated that she wanted to be transferred to Sweden and remain incarcerated there in order to be closer to her family. Her mother returned to Sweden, and she couldn't visit her often in a California prison.

California Government Code regulates the transfer of prisoners and only a Governor, or an executive officer of the Board of Parole Hearings can approve a transfer of a prisoner. Back in 2007, Swedish Prime Minister Fredrik Reinfeldt met Governor Arnold Schwarzenegger and tried to convince him to transfer Östberg back to her home country, but the Governor ignored the request. Sweden's diplomats continued to work on the case and managed to move it from a standstill. Her transfer progressed quickly, and she was back in Sweden after only a couple of months.

This led to a lot of speculation about what really made the Board of Parole change their minds. Some suspected that a financial crisis which was shaking the country at the time was the reason why the United States agreed to send Annika back to Sweden. With so many prisoners behind the bars, it is a real burden to take a good care of them. So the United States saw this as a favor because they would have one criminal less in their facilities.

After arriving in Sweden, Annika Östberg was once again incarcerated, but the exact duration of her sentence was unknown. The Swedish Court discussed the case in November 2009, and they decided to keep her in prison until May of 2011. Numerous news crews interviewed Annika as soon as she returned to Sweden.

Swedish authorities would set Annika free in on May 2nd, 2011. She reconnected with her mother, and the two of them managed to repair their relationship. Annika's mother lives in a retirement home now, and the two of them see each other all the time. Annika remains the only Swedish citizen that served a sentence of thirty years in prison.

SERIAL KILLING STRIPPER: THE TRUE STORY OF ROBYN LINDHOLM

CHELSEA CALBERT
Australia's Most Dangerous Woman

Robyn Lindholm was destined for fame. By the age of 14, this talented, beautiful young woman was already an up-and-comer in the world of Australian figure skating – competing in national ice-skating championships and even performing alongside Olympic legends Torvill and Dean, handpicked by the duo to participate in their sold-out Face The Music world tour.

However, it wasn't her talent on the ice that ensured Lindholm's name would appear on the front page of newspapers for years. Instead, this gorgeous femme fatale will be remembered as a murderer – and potentially, even a serial killer.

The Victorian Supreme Court finally sentenced 43-year-old Lindholm to 25 years in prison for the premeditated murder of her ex-boyfriend, Wayne Amey, in December of 2015 – but then, police began investigating the possibility that Lindholm was behind at least one other death, as well as the possible murder of another past lover.

"She had an uncanny ability to manipulate men," said Chief Crown Prosecutor Gavin Silbert QC, during one of Lindholm's trials.

Always daddy's girl

Born into a wealthy Melbourne family, Lindholm learned at an early age that her good looks and charm could get her anything she wanted. Even her father was powerless to resist. At the age of 11, Lindholm convinced him that she needed a pony. A few years later, a 14-year-old Lindholm demanded pricey skating lessons – and her dad never failed to indulge his daughter's every wish.

While Lindholm relied heavily on her appearance to get ahead, she grew up a fairly hardworking young girl. After excelling at Kilvington Grammar and even at an elite secondary college, Lindholm planned to attend Monash University to study a Bachelor of Science degree. Her love of horses had endured since childhood, and her passion for endurance riding led Lindholm to pursue a career working with animals.

Her bright future began to derail when she accepted a part-time job working in one of the high-roller rooms at the Crown Casino, the Mahogany Room. Even though Lindholm was just a hostess, her long legs and beautiful blonde hair caught the eye of "the Black Prince of Lygon Street." Alphonse Gangitano was an attractive and wealthy underworld crime leader, and Lindholm was unable to resist the allure of the handsome and powerful man's lifestyle of money, sex, and drugs.

Lindholm's demanding nature suited Gangitano just fine. Once again, she was treated like a princess – Gangitano was more than willing to indulge Lindholm's every whim and buy her whatever she desired. When Gangitano was eventually executed in his own home, Lindholm would need to find another way to maintain the intoxicating lifestyle she'd gotten accustomed to – by whatever means necessary.

Simply Irresistible

While working in the Mahogany Room, Lindholm had developed a relationship with Alex Prelac – a regular customer of the exclusive high-roller room who owned the Simply Irresistible Stripping Agency. Lindholm had purchased her first small farm in Glenhope when she was only 23, and agreed to work part-time for Prelac's agency to help pay down her mortgage.

Stripping not only provided Lindholm with a steady income and the exciting lifestyle she was looking for – it also indulged her need to be the centre of attention. Her job with Simply Irresistible wasn't enough, though. Soon, Lindholm made the jump from stripping to working back in Melbourne's underworld as a highly-paid escort, going by the name "Collette."

John Elder, who worked as editor-in-chief of a magazine that routinely hired strippers for pranks and other comical roles, recalled meeting Lindholm when she was only 20 years old – "an ice-skating champion, newly dropped out of a science degree, moving into animal husbandry."

"She talked to me about her dream of owning her own place in the country, horses, a quiet life," he said. "There was nothing to suggest she'd end up burying one, maybe two boyfriends at the wished-for homestead."

Elder added that for Lindholm, stripping was a "means to a real-estate end," and that as soon as she was able to save enough money, she'd move on to her real passion of working with horses.

Soon after she started at the club, Lindholm struck up a close friendship with another stripper, Shari Davison. Davison was an exotic dancer who had previously worked as a circus trapeze artist, and who had just had a baby when she disappeared after leaving the Crown Casino on a Saturday morning in February of 1995. Her body has never been recovered, but investigations soon began to point to her good friend, Lindholm.

"There were so many rumours, ratbags, and depraved offshoots in our digging around," Elder said. "An inquest in 2001 found that Davison had a taste for drugs, booze, and bad men – and was pronounced mysteriously dead."

Apparently, in the weeks leading up to her disappearance, Davison had confessed to some close friends that she was "in serious trouble" with a gang of young Greeks – a gang which included standover man George Teazis, who had recently started seeing a stripper known as "Collette."

Teazis, also known as Templeton, had once been a member of a Richmond-based gang. The gang participated in the trading of weapons and amphetamines, dubbed the "plastic gangsters." Teazis fell head over heels in love with Lindhom, and even went as far to propose to her and move her into his home. However, he vanished in 2005, shortly after the engagement, and his body remains unfound.

A volatile situation

Two weeks prior to his disappearance, Teazis's brother received an upsetting phone call. Teazis was in tears, distraught over having just caught Lindholm in bed with, presumably, Wayne Amey. According to the brother, the couple had a "violent fight," and Teazis decided to leave Lindholm.

On the day Teazis disappeared, Lindholm had been out with a friend. When she came home, she claims the door was open and Teazis was gone. According to Lindholm, Teazis had sent a text at around 2:30am, stating that he was in some kind of trouble and would need a ride home, but she didn't know where he was.

Tearfully, Lindholm took to the press to express her pain and desire to locate her beloved fiancé. In the meantime, though, she moved all the furniture out of Teazis' home and claimed all of his assets – leaving a small box of toys for her fiancé's grief-stricken teenage son, Ross.

"Ross noticed that his father's F100 campervan was missing, along with his motorbike, a boat, a rear-projection television, jewellery, and other assorted goods worth an uncounted tens of thousands of dollars," said Elder. "Ross says he was so stunned at the time, he immediately went to a friend's home to settle himself. Later, he tried calling (Lindholm), to claim his father's belongings."

According to Ross, Lindholm eventually texted to tell him that she'd left some "clothes and his remote-controlled cars" in boxes on the doorstep. When Ross inquired about the vehicles, Lindholm replied that he would be "getting nothing … and she forwarded her solicitor's details."

And while Lindholm made a show of crying for the press, Teazis' family members claimed that before getting in front of the cameras, Lindholm had been "laughing with her friend." After shedding some tears during the press conference and mourning the disappearance of her lover, she was "seen laughing again when it was over."

She also chose not to mention her new lover to the TV and newspaper reporters. Before Teazis' disappearance, Lindholm had started an affair with a gym owner named Wayne Amey. With Teazis out of the picture and her stripping career taking off, Lindholm was on track to get everything she ever wanted.

Lindholm reluctanty sold her Glenhope farm to purchase land with Amey, a 10-acre property near Bittern. This would give her plenty of space to pursue her lasting love of equestrianism and, eventually, begin breeding horses. Up until her arrest, Lindholm continued to enjoy endurance riding, and at the time Amey was killed, their property was home to eight beautiful – and expensive – Arabian horses.

Lady Macbeth in Lycra

Although 'Teazis' body was never recovered, Lindholm was formally charged with his murder in June of 2016. In 2005, police had conceded that it was possible that Teazis may not have wanted to ever be found – but since he hadn't used his mobile phone or accessed his bank accounts, they had "grave concerns."

According to police, Lindholm had convinced her new lover, Amey, to help her kill and dispose of her fiancé – a story that was somewhat corroborated by a strip club owner who had hired Amey as a personal trainer.

"He said (Teazis) was knocking Robyn around," she told Elder. "He kept saying he was going to kill (Teazis). It went on and on. It got scary and I stopped training with him."

The charge came just a few months after Lindholm was convicted of persuading another lover, Torsten "Toots" Trabert, to murder Amey. According to Elder, Lindholm and Amey were separating – and Amey had hoped for a settlement that would leave him half of the couple's rural property.

"Lindholm was angry, vengeful, and bitter over the break-up of her relationship with Amey and the loss of the farm, and he became anxious for his own safety," said a newspaper article published in The Sunday Age, discussing the case.

According to defence barrister John Kelly, Lindholm had "lost everything." Unemployed and living out of her car, she decided her only option was to kill Amey – a man she'd once hoped to start a family with.

"Her sense of grievance at the situation she found herself in needs to be viewed through that prism," Kelly told the Supreme Court following Lindholm's plea of guilt. "She had lost all sense of proportion at that stage. But she blamed Amey for the straights she was in because ... she says she had the most wonderful upbringing and childhood she could hope to have."

Kelly added that by 2013, Lindholm was a "40-year-old woman with no prospect that she could see, no means of support, and no property or assets to her name," but added that none of this information "ameliorates what then happened to Amey."

Despite her desire to see Amey killed, Lindholm knew wouldn't be able to commit the murder on her own. If she wanted her ex-lover dead, she'd need to convince her new lover to do the dirty work. While Lindholm considered her relationship with Trabert to be nothing more than a "fling," he had fallen "madly in love."

"Trabert was infatuated with her," said Chief Crown Prosecutor Gavin Silbert QC, noting that the pair were involved in an "intense sexual relationship." He added that Trabert had even left his wife and children to move in with Lindholm – but there was a price to be paid.

"He couldn't keep his hands off her, and the return for her affection was that he kill Wayne Amey," Silbert said. "It was only with the seduction of Travert that she achieved her aims."

According to Silbert, Trabert wasn't Lindholm's first choice. In fact, he told the Victorian Supreme Court during Lindholm's trial that the stripper had attempted to convince several other former lovers to help her get rid of Amey, but Trabert was the first one to agree to her plan.

However, Trabert did need a bit of persuading. Silbert told the court that Lindholm used her sexuality to seduce Trabert into doing her bidding – to the point where, Silbert said, Trabert was completely obsessed with her. Even while locked in a remand cell following his arrest, Trabert sent flowery love notes to "darling" Lindholm.

"I'm missing you so much that I can't sleep because you are not with me ... we are so good together," one note read. "I can't think of my life without. All my love, Toots."

Trabert ended his note with a carefully drawn heart containing the words "I love you forever."

According to plan

The murder was carried out on December 10, 2013 – the day before Amey and Lindholm were due in court to resolve their dispute over a $1.1 million rural property they owned in Bittern. Lindholm directed Trabert and his accomplice, John Anthony Ryan, to attack Amey at his apartment.

The two men beat him repeatedly with a baseball bat, stabbed him, and choked him – and then wrapped him up and stuffed him in the trunk of the car. The group then drove to a remote farm in Mt Korong in Central Victoria, to get rid of Amey's body.

According to court reports, Trabert had tried to find a fourth person to help the trio "finish off" Amey, but this person refused to get involved. At this point, records state, Amey could be heard "begging for his life" from the trunk of the car. When the car was parked at the farm, Trabert and Ryan completed the murder.

"Post-mortem examination revealed that Amey had multiple stab injuries to his chest, fractured ribs, pallor and furrow to the left side of his neck in association with a rope, and multiple lacerations to his scalp," the court records revealed. "The opinion of the forensic pathologist was that Amey's death was a result of one or more of these injuries."

Lindholm kept a watchful eye on her suitor as he and Ryan pushed the body into a crevice between two rocks, ordering them to use more rocks and sticks to cover Amey's corpse and ensure it wouldn't be discovered.

Once the body was sufficiently hidden, Lindholm and Trabert had sex in the bushes, while Ryan went to a nearby Inglewood hotel to meet them for drinks. The trio attempted to use Amey's bank cards to clean out his accounts, and eventually set his vehicle on fire to destroy any remaining evidence.

"(Lindholm) was laughing and carrying on like it was nothing," Ryan told police. "She's on top of the world. They just wanted to f—-ing party, and I just felt ill, ill the whole way."

Charges laid

Lindholm, Trabert, and Ryan were all apprehended by police just days after Amey's murder. A car pursuit between Trabert, Lindholm, and police ended on foot – Trabert was nabbed by police, while Lindholm attempted evade them by crossing a creek. Ryan, meanwhile, was apprehended at a residential address in Coburg after the body was discovered.

"We have found Amey on the top of a hill," said Sen-Constable Philip Gynther, leading homicide detective on the case. "His remains have been place at the bottom of a crevasse between two large rocks. It's been a very long process ... the terrain all looks very similar."

According to court documents, Lindholm pleaded guilty to Amey's murder, while Trabert and Ryan plead their innocence – "each maintaining that it was the other who had killed Amey."

All three received sentences from Supreme Court Justice Lex Lasry – 25 years for Lindholm, 28 years for Trabert, and 31 years for Ryan. According to Lasry, Lindholm had shown "no remorse" for her role in Amey's murder – saying she "no doubt" felt ashamed and embarrassed, but he didn't believe she had a genuine regret for her "bizarre actions" in the "appalling crime."

Lasry also stated the trio had a history of "excessive use" of crystal meth – a drug which tends to fuel "extraordinarily violent criminal behaviour," he said.

While appeals were submitted for reduced terms, Senior Crown prosecutor Douglas Trapnell, QC, said each member of the trio was "equally responsible" for their roles in Amey's murder – whether as an instigator or as a physical killer.

"Because this was a pre-meditated plan and callous killing on the eve of a court hearing, where Amey was to exercise his legal rights, brings it very close to the worst case," Trapnell said. "This man was beaten in the basement of his apartment building where he had the right to feel safe. He was hog-tied ... then put in (a car) boot and remained alive for quite some time, albeit with (injuries including) fractured ribs."

Trapnell also argued that the trio had "desecrated" Amey's body by stuffing it into the crevice on Mt Korong, where, without the assistance of Trabert, it might never have been located. Following his apprehension, Trabert had led police to the farm where Amey's body had been hidden.

"The location of the body by my client allowed the family to seek some closure in having the body returned and afforded a proper burial," said Trabert's lawyer, Adam Chernok. "It's arguable it would have been a much more difficult case to prove and indeed may not have obtained the plea of Lindholm."

Chernok added that while Lindholm had a "primary motive" to kill her lover, his client's only motive was "put very simply, your honour, sex."

"If the killing of Amey is Lindholm's wicked design, it is not a truly shared motive in terms of the killing as I've described," Chernok said. "My client is motivated by sex in the context of his particular circumstances."

David Hallowes, who defended Ryan, claimed his client didn't become involved in the plot until after he'd been told that Amey was "mistreating" Lindholm. According to Hallowes, Ryan had believed the plan was only to "beat" Amey – and that without Lindholm's participation, the murder would never have happened.

However, according to Justice Philip Priest, the two men had ample opportunity to back out of the plan while Amey was still alive in the trunk of the car. The fact that they continued with the murder shows "how nasty this killing was."

"Lindholm sought to bring about Amey's murder for two years," stated the judgment from the Court of Appeal in October of 2016, dismissing the bid from the trio. "She tried to persuade others to kill him for her, and eventually, she persuaded Trabert to do it. Trabert and Ryan callously, ruthlessly, and violently carried out her wishes."

In fact, the statement added that Lindholm had continued to arrange for Amey's murder even after she'd broken into his apartment and received a community corrections order. According to court records, Lindholm and others had conducted surveillance on Amey, and she'd broken into the apartment even though she had a swipe card that could have been used to gain entry.

Records show she had told an associate that she'd done this so that "if something happened in the future, it would look like she did not have access to the property."

"It is difficult to overstate Lindholm's moral culpability for this crime," the court said. "She pleaded guilty but the (sentencing) judge found that she was not remorseful. In our view, the sentence imposed on her was a merciful one in the circumstances."

More than sex on legs

Supporting the charges were a series of text messages exchanged between Lindholm and Amey in the weeks leading up to his murder, included as part of the police evidence against Lindholm.

"Look at that ring on your finger Rob," read one message from Amey to Lindholm. "The one I designed, had made and ask you to marry me with, AND I MEANT IT. What better chance could anyone get? You cheated on that ring and me. Remember that when it's on your finger next time you sleep with him."

"Wayne you wouldn't take me back. I tried for months," said one of Lindholm's texts to Amey. "After I recognized my mistakes you still rejected me. I was only good enough to f—k. That was all. When I f—-ked up I was in a bad place lonely and messed up. I know that hurt and I don't know why I did it but the last few months when I begged to come home and I wanted you more than anything you still rejected me continuously. And took everything away."

"I need to feel like I'm more than just sex on legs," she said. "There's Robyn here too not just Collette."

Another text from Amey stated that Lindholm had gotten herself "in this position from a LIFETIME of lies, deception, drug abuse, selfishness and hate."And in another message to Amey, Lindholm told him that if he made her life any more difficult than he already had, "you will regret it Wayne."

According to Lindholm, the couple had been drifting apart for years. By the time their relationship started, Lindholm was in her 30s – ready to get married and start a family. Amey, though, already had a son from a previous relationship and decided to get a vasectomy. According to Amey, the couple "couldn't afford" a child because of their outstanding debts.

By 2009, Lindholm was even more frustrated with her relationship with Amey. He'd promised to retire with her at the Bittern property following his 50th birthday – but that never happened.

"She anticipated that the pair of them would live out there and she would raise her horses out there and they would see out their twilight years together there," said Kelly, Lindholm's lawyer.

Officially, the pair split in 2011, but according to Lindholm, Amey continued to reach out to her for casual sex, right up until his death.

"He was very into that and whenever he got drunk or smashed he used to call me and that was right up until not long ago," Lindholm told police after Amey was killed. "We used to do a lot of threesomes and he used to get me to bring girls home a lot."

However, despite what Ryan had been told about Amey "mistreating" Lindholm, she told police their relationship had never been violent. In fact, she claimed Amey was "kind" to her.

"We loved each other, but we just grew apart," she said. "I would never let anyone hurt (Amey) because he's never hurt me. He was always good to me."

An average guy

According to Amey's teammates from the Camberwell Hockey Club, he was happy, friendly guy – who happened to get in with a "fast crowd." While he wasn't known for sharing many details about his personal life, he had broached the topic of his relationship with Lindholm about three week before he was killed.

Amey had felt as though a weight had been lifted from his shoulders, believing that his dispute with Lindholm over the Bittern property was coming to an end – it was finally on the market, and once the property sold, Amey would be able to get a brand-new start.

"He spoke openly about a breakup some time ago that had turned sour and threatening," said Dugald Jellie, a teammate from the hockey club. "(Amey) was caught in a drama he couldn't undo. He'd tried restraining orders. He wanted only to quit his ex-partner and her friends, sell his country retreat, then one day sell his gym and start anew."

As a youth, Amey had been a top-grade hockey player. As an adult, he'd taken to playing in Camberwell's veteran's squad and working with the club to help develop its younger players. Jellie was one of his hockey mates, who had traveled with Amey to a game in Geelong just a few weeks before he was murdered. He was deeply affected by the news of Amey's death.

"It frightens me to think of (Amey) being hurt and in such peril. It is awful to think of him being so vulnerable, so helpless, so in need of his friends when none of us were there," Jellie said. "I can't stop but think of the moment he was jumped, and of his fears, and how alone he must have felt."

Active investigation

While serving her 25-year sentence for arranging Amey's murder, Lindholm received a new set of charges in June 2016 – naming her responsible for the murder of George Teazis, back in 2005. Appearing before the Melbourne Magistrate's Court via video link from the notorious Dame Phyllis Frost Centre women's prison, Lindholm refused to enter a plea, or speak at all, other than to confirm her name to the magistrate.

In 2017, defence counsel will hold a committal hearing and plan to cross-examine more than 20 witnesses, which will determine if Lindholm will then stand trial.

Investigations are ongoing to determine the extent of Lindholm's possible involvement in the disappearance of Shari Davison, as well.

KILLER SEDUCTRESS

GARY RACE

Shayna Hubers

Shayna Hubers is a 21-year-old graduate from Lexington, Kentucky. She grew up in a comfortably middle-class family and was a smart young woman. She graduated from Paul Laurence Dunbar High School in 2009, and went on to college. During high school, Shayna's friends described her as quiet and "most likely to succeed". Shayna graduated from Kentucky's prestigious School of the Arts after making Dean's list in 2012. She was in the process of pursuing a Master's Degree in counseling from Eastern Kentucky University when she took the life of her on-again off-again boyfriend, Ryan Poston and effectively put her life on hold.

Poston was a 29-year-old lawyer and business owner from a successful family of attorneys and executives. He was loved by his friends and family and admired by women. He was known to be friendly, respectful and respectable, and an overall good guy. He met Hubers in 2011 through mutual friends on Facebook and the attraction was instantaneous, as the first photos of Hubers that Poston saw were racy in nature. The two began to chat, and started officially dating shortly after they went on their first date. They continued their relationship for over a year. If it hadn't been for Facebook, the two more than likely never would have met, as Shayna lived 80 miles away from Ryan and had no reason to venture into Ryan's neck of the woods.

Throughout the entirety of the relationship, the couple sent thousands of text messages, including a conversation about possibly taking a two-week long break from each other and the relationship. Hubers was also known to post pictures of herself and Poston on Instagram. The seemingly happy couple exchanged over a thousand photo messages, as well as 20,000 messages through Facebook. Most of the Facebook messages had been sent by Hubers to Poston, who had responded to only a handful of them.

To people who weren't aware of the couple's dynamics, it appeared as if they were a happy couple who had everything going for them. They were both beautiful, successful, and driven. It was a match made in heaven- or so it appeared to be, but the truth was much darker and would become the subject of a complicated trial and a life term in prison.

On October 11, 2012, Hubers and Poston and his family had dinner at the young lawyer's home. After dinner, Hubers went home- she returned a few hours later, however, and the couple got into a heated argument. Poston informed his girlfriend that he wanted to end their 18-month long relationship, and it set Hubers off into a fit of anger. Her anger worsened when she was later told that Poston already had a date lined up with the 2012 Miss Ohio, Audrey Bolte. It's believed that the news of Ryan's new date was what pushed Hubers over the edge.

In the morning, Hubers' mother drove two hours to pick up her daughter and the two went out shopping. They were out for most of the day before Shayna was dropped back off at Ryan's house, telling her mother that she wanted to stay with him. Despite her other asking her numerous times to come home with her, Hubers was adamant that she wanted to stay at Poston's house. Shortly after, Poston became aware that Shayna was planning to stay at his place- he used this time to inform her that he had another date and didn't intend to spend the night with her. By 9 o'clock that night, the young lawyer was dead on his dining room floor.

At 8:53 that chilly Friday night, Hubers placed a 911 call from Poston's condo and said to the responding dispatcher: "Ma'am, I have...I have...I have killed my boyfriend in self-defense".

The dispatcher then asked what happened, to which Hubers replied "He beat me and tried to carry me out of the house and I came back in to get my stuff. He was right in front of me and reached down to grab the gun. I grabbed it out of his hands and pulled the trigger".

The dispatcher then instructed Hubers to step outside with her hands in front of her. Hubers complied, and responding officer, David Fornash's partner cuffed and took her away while Fornash himself went to investigate the crime scene.

Fornash and the other officers who responded to the scene, found Ryan Poston lying on his dining room floor next to a Sig Sauer .380-caliber pistol. The pistol, upon further inspection, was found to have belonged to Poston, who had a passion for guns. "...he would have them in his boot, he would have them in his holster..." says Poston's ex-girlfriend, Lauren Whorley, who claimed that Poston's love of guns made her feel safe.

Fornash went room to room, double checking that there were no other hiding in the apartment and upon finding Poston's body, officers found that he had been shot once in the back, twice in the head, and three times in his upper body. The coroner is called and Fornash sets off for the station where Hubers had been escorted into an interrogation room and sat waiting.

Meanwhile Poston, lying dead on his kitchen floor, was supposed to meet with Audrey Bolte at the Milford Inn bar for a night of drinks and harmless flirting. Poston, however, did not show up and Bolte went home feeling confused. When asked how she felt about him not showing up, Bolte said that it was odd for Poston not to show up or give some sort of notice that he wasn't coming, as he was a very responsible individual.

Friends of Poston claim that he and Hubers were never really in a committed relationship, as Poston lost interest in Hubers rather quickly and made several halfhearted attempts to break it off with her. In fact, by October of 2012, Ryan had made 3 attempts to sever Shayna's ties to him. According to text messages between Poston and his cousin, he was emotionally drained from dealing with Shayna. "I received 75 text messages from her. I am emotionally and mentally spent. I hope she leaves me alone" reads one message between the cousins. Despite this, Poston continued to go out with Hubers and pose for photos.

Shayna, confiding in a friend through text messages, said that Poston had told her that he's only with her because he felt bad when she cries. She is also quoted as saying: "My love has turned to hate."

In one particularly chilling message Shayna claims that "...tonight when I go to the shooting range with Ryan, I want to turn around, shoot, and kill him, and play like it's an accident." The next day, Shayna posts a photo of herself with a gun at the shooting range.

The night of the murder, Shayna was interviewed about the incident. Left alone in the interogation room, Shayne almost seemed proud of what she had done, reports Chief Bill Birkenhauer. He watched her on live camera snapping her fingers, dancing around, and muttering to herself "I killed him, I killed him."

Legally, officers were not allowed to interrogate her without an attorney present, so when she was brought into the interview room they didn't ask any questions. In fact, officers didn't say anything. Shayna, however, readily volunteered her story of how the events took place. She was rambling on for two hours before running out of things to say. According to officers, the men and women who took turns sitting with Shayna, quickly grew tired of her rambling and would have preferred to leave. "Shayna appeared to be nervous, or trying to cover something up" one officer said. "...her stories, after a while, stopped matching up and kept changing." This, according to the officer, might have been happening as a result of Shayna realizing that she was in over her head.

When speaking about Poston's death, Hubers said that she knew he was dead because he was twitching. Her exact words were: "Literally, that's when I knew that he was dead or close to it...the twitching...and that was it." She goes on to explain how she couldn't let him sit there and twitch. She couldn't stand to sit there and watch him die so she shot 5 more rounds into his body to finish him off.

In addition to building a case of self-defense and trying to convince officers that she deeply loved Ryan, she claims that "he was very vain...he wants to get a nose job...I shot him right here-" she pointed to her nose and continued her story "...and I gave him the nose job that he wanted."

Officers didn't buy Shayna's claims of self defense due to lack of evidence that Poston was ever abusive towards her. "She claimed that she was pushed and that he hit her, however, there were no visible marks or wounds at all on any part of Shayna's body" says former FBI profiler James Fitzgerald.

"There was no evidence in Ryan's condo that there was a fight" adds Laura Richards, a prominent criminal behavioral analyst.

Photos from the crime scene show evidence against Shayna's claims of a fight, as there were a number of pill bottles and bullets standing on end on the table. Had a fight taken place, they would have been knocked over or displaced and the murder area would have been left a mess. Instead, it was neat and tidy other than the pool of Ryan's blood that was left behind after the shooting. Shayna had also claimed that Poston had thrown her against a bookshelf. The bookshelf in question, when police arrived, was undisturbed.

As for Shayna's odd behavior when left alone, Richards believes that it was an act in an attempt to appear mentally unstable and open the door for the insanity plea should her self-defense claims fall short. "She couldn't decide which plea to go with- self-defense or insanity. So, she decided to open the doors to both and see which one panned out the best."

After three hours of deliberation, Shayna is charged with one count of first degree murder. In 2014, her trial is well underway and a forensic pathologist mentions that at the time he was shot, Poston had been sitting down- a fact that goes against what Shayna had said previously. According to Richards, this fact alone blows Shayna's claims of self-defense out the window as it shows that Ryan was not charging at her in a fit of rage, as she had previously claimed. Instead, he had been seated and had been seated great distance away from Shayna at the time of the murder. Forensic expert Howard Ryan backs this theory up by going into detail about the shots that Shayna fired at Poston. He says that the first shot was to Poston's head, a fact that is significant due to the lack of blood found on Ryan's shirt.

"If he had been standing up, the gravity would have brought it down...straight down the shirt through the bottom to the pants" he says.

Using the blood stains on the table, Ryan is able to provide further detail as to why he believes that Poston was sitting down. "When she shoots him in the forehead, his head goes down on the table." Poston's head would not have fallen onto the table if he had been in an upright position. From here, Ryan suspects that Poston's back was left exposed, setting him up for the next shot. At the same time that he is being shot a second time, his right arms falls limp and opens up the area of his body that will receive the third shot- which is right underneath of his arm. After this, his body slumps to the floor and remains there until it is removed by the coroner.

Three of Shayna's cellmates testified against her that day, claiming that she had told them that she intended to kill Ryan that night and that he had never been abusive to her. "She laughed about shooting him in the face and giving him the nose job he always wanted" claims Cecily Miller.

Another inmate, Holly Nivens, claims that Shayna made the whole abuse story up. When speaking about the bruises and scratches that Shayna would show people, Nivens claimed that Shayna inflicted them on herself.

Shayna also told her cellmates that she had messed the apartment up and thrown objects around to make it appear as though a vicious fight had taken place.

Shayna didn't take the stand, but prosecutors used her social media and interview footage as a substitution. Despite the overwhelming evidence against Hubers, her defense team maintained its argument that Poston had been abusive and that Shayna had acted out of self defense when she shot him.

A toxicologist was asked to plead in Shayna's defense and said that at the time of his death, Ryan had a strong mix of Xanax and Adderall in his system. He argues that these medications could have caused outbursts of anger and violence, making it possible for Ryan to snap and come after Hubers with a both his fists and then later on, a deadly weapon such as a gun.

A clinical psychologist was also called to testify on her behalf, and he diagnosed her with bipolar disorder with narcissistic tenancies, and post traumatic stress disorder (PTSD).

"She was very distraught. She was depressed" says the psychologist who claims that Shayna had told him that she had suffered from sexual abuse as a child, and was recognized as having alcohol and prescription drug abuse issues.

On the day of the trial, Shayna painted herself as a model girl friend to Poston, claiming that he had been going through a lot and that she had always been there for moral support.

"I was always good to him" she said.

Again, the jury didn't buy the story. Five hours after her trial started, Shayna was officially charged. She appeared back in court three months later for sentencing and was given 40 years behind bars. Shayna's defense team tried to lower the time before she becomes eligible for parole to 8 years instead of 20, but was denied this motion.

Just six months later, her legal team filed another motion seeking a new trial. According to her team, one of the jurors who convicted

Shayna had not been legally eligible to convict her as he was a convicted felon himself. This, according to Kentucky law, made him unable to serve the court and gave Shayna's legal team a reason for a new trial.

It's said that Shayna's new trial date is set for early 2018. Until then, she is behind bars and serving her 40 year sentence as planned.

The new trial was originally set for January of 2018, but has been put on hold for 4 months longer at the request of Shayna's legal team. The extra time, according to her attorney, will be used to prepare.

Despite the 40 year sentence, Ryan's friends and loved ones are left with a sour taste in their mouths. Lauren Whorley, in an interview with a news station, claims that she wishes she would have known what was going on- maybe then she would have been able to help and prevent Ryan from getting too tangled up in Hubers. She also said that she believes the trial should have been handled in an "an eye for an eye" fashion, meaning that what Shayna did to Ryan, should have been done back to her as justice.

"Maybe it's traditional, old-school mentality, but if you kill someone, then you know, it's an eye for an eye. And what you due unto others should be done unto you" she said.

For her, however, the sentencing brought a sliver of much appreciated peace. "I was there when they read it" she said about the final verdict "It was the longest 30 seconds of my life."

Matt Herren, a close friend of Ryan, still struggles to make sense of what went wrong that night. "I think about him everyday," he says "You just don't think something like that will happen to someone you know."

Like Whorley, Matt wonders if there is something he could have done to prevent Ryan from suffering the fate he did. "I know a lot of people in his life feel the same way" he says to "48 Hours" correspondent Peter Van Sant.

Van Sant asked Herren what was lost when Ryan was killed and Herren responded with "He's the type of person you want in your life. Not just a friend, but a loving son, a protective, older brother. He had three younger sisters that he adored." Poston had cared deeply for his three younger sisters and only ever wanted the best for them. In return, they showered him with love and looked up to their older brother.

Ryan and his family had been close-knit, despite his mom and dad divorcing when he was a child. He was close to his father, and when his mother remarried, he grew an attachment to his new step-father, Peter Carter. Ryan thought of him as a second father.

According to Sarah Robinson, a woman who had grown up with Shayna, her future had seemed promising as well. Shayna had been a good student and was never in any trouble.

"I thought she was, close to genius, in my opinion" she said " I mean, she was always in AP classes. Always getting A's in everything."

During her academic career, Hubers had received various awards for academic excellence and leadership.

"She liked to succeed at anything and everything she did" Robinson concludes.

When Van Sant asked her what Shayna had been like with boys in high school, Robinson mentioned that Shayna could be dramatic. "If a guy, broke up with her or something, she would take it pretty hard" she explained "...crying, and a maybe a bit of screaming..she didn't really like to let things go."

When asked if Shayna had been happy with Ryan, Robinson said that as far as she knew, she had been. As far as she knew, they had both been happy.

Ryan's friend, Allie Wagner, claimed that there was something wrong with the relationship from the start when she was asked the same question about Ryan. According to Wagner, Shayna had been cold upon their first meeting. "You could just immediately tell that...that she was obsessed with him," she says.

"He was busy with work..he didn't really have time for anyone" Herren adds. "He didn't want to hurt her feelings..that wasn't the kind of person he was."

As Shayna's denial towards Ryan's disinterest progressed, he started to wonder if he might need to put a restraining order out against her. "This is getting to be restraining order level crazy..." he wrote in a text message to his cousin "She's shown up at my condo 3 times and refuses to leave each time."

Ryan's neighbor, Nikki Carnes claims that there may have been two sides to the tumultuous relationship. She says that Ryan may have been emotionally abusive. According to Carnes, Shayna complained frequently of Ryan putting her down. "She told me that he would say she needed a boob job or a face lift and that she was fat and needed to lose some weight" she says.

Van Sant then asked her why Shayna wouldn't have left and she replied "I guess because she was young and she always told me she loved him." Carnes also told Van Sant that Shayna did everything for Ryan from taking his dog outside to picking up and doing his laundry. On the night of the shooting, she also reportedly heard gunshots but didn't hear the couple fighting, as Shayna had claimed that they had.

Wagner, when asked what she thought could have happened that night replied, "I think she went over there...tried to talk him out of breaking up with her. And I think he just stood his ground for the first time," she said "I think he just said no, like, this isn't working. So she picked up the gun and shot him."

Chief Birkenhauer agreed with Wagner's theory "He wanted to break up with her...I think that Shayna was not gonna be broken up with" he said in an interview with Van Sant.

Prosecutor Michelle Snodgrass explains why Shayna's pleas of abuse were dismissed. "Someone who is in shock does not pirouette," she says in response to the police videos of Shayna singing and dancing in the interview room "Within hours of putting six bullets in Ryan Poston and watching him die, she was dancing and singing."

"There were hundreds of thousands of text messages. And most of them were from Shayna. For every 1 message Ryan sent, she sent probably 50," Snodgrass says "She couldn't stop herself."

According to Snodgrass, rejection was what ultimately pushed Shayna over the edge and drove her to kill the man she so desperately loved.

"Ryan's a bright guy; he's a lawyer" says Van Sant to Snodgrass "Why wouldn't he get a restraining order?"

"Under the law in Kentucky, he didn't qualify for a restraining order. The law in Kentucky required the two to have been living together or to have been married" she replied.

Van Sant then spoke to Hubers' mother, Sharon, about the tragedy. "She graduated cum laude in three years at the University of Kentucky. She was pursuing a Master's Degree in school guidance counseling," she said.

"And what do you want people to know after reading this" Van Sant asked "...in relation to this case?"

"Shayna Hubers is not a child, a girl, a person that would murder someone; that would wake up and say 'OK, I'm going to shoot somebody"

"I want the world to know who Shayna is. And I want them to hear it from her mother" she concludes tearfully.

Hubers and her mother had been close most of Shayna's life, according to Sarah Robinson. "I think she was very close to her mom. I think her mom, for a good portion of her life, could have been her best friend."

This statement is backed up by a quote from Sharon Hubers in her interview with Van Sant: "That child has been a blessing to me. She's my whole life."

"The word that has been used to describe your daughter is evil" Van Sant teold Sharon.

"She's far from evil. Shayna has a heart of gold. She's like her mommy...a loving spirit. That's what I want the world to know" she replied.

After the trial, Shayna spoke up for the first time. Despite having killed their beloved family member, she didn't apologize to Poston's family. Instead, she apologized to her family and friends, and speaks only of herself.

"I'm sorry to my family. And I'm sorry to my friends for letting them down. And I'm sorry for the money my parents had to spend on attorneys" she says, after being convicted of the murder.

"I do wanna help people. I do wanna be something better. And I do want to continue to grow and learn" she said to the judge "And I just don't think a 40 year sentence will help me. I don't think it would benefit me any."

Judge Fred Stine replied to Shayna's statement with his own choice words. "What I think happened in that apartment was little more than cold-blooded murder."

Regardless of what happened that night, a promising young lawyer lays dead, and a successful college student sits rotting behind bars. Two families have been destroyed, and law officials are left baffled. Both the victim and offender have been robbed of their lives- and for what? For a reason that the offender calls love.

Killer Seductress : Pamela Smart

Sarah Thompson

The case of Pamela Smart is infamous and retold in popular media through episodes on crime-based drama. What is it about Pamela Smart and her affair with a fifteen-year-old boy that draws society to continue to retell her case? The murder of Gregory Smart, Pamela's husband, is one that tells a story not often seen in the trends of women who commit murder.

Women who kill are so statistically and socially interesting to us that we, as a society, often gather up their specific stories into anthologies and special documentaries. Television shows like "Snapped" and "Deadly Women" focus exclusively on female cases of murder. Meanwhile, television shows that have been going on since the early nineties, like "Forensics Files", have an overwhelming number of male offenders. Of course, this isn't to say that women are incapable of murder, or that they do so infrequently. In fact, statistics have proved that women are entirely capable of killing, and often do so.

Information gathered by the Bureau of Justice Statistics, with data gathered between 1976 and 1997, shows the rate of murder committed by females was about 1.3 per 100,000. That is to say, for every 77,000 women, one would end up to be a murderer. The victims, in this case, were overwhelmingly the spouse. 60,000 murders were committed by women between the years of 1976 and 1997, and 60% of the victims were an intimate partner or family member.

While these numbers may be shocking, the context of the killings is also important. For example, 92% of all women in California prisons are estimated to have been battered or abused by either the spouse, intimate partner, or family member at some point in their lives. In 1992, data gathered by the Georgia Department of Corrections showed that of the 235 women that were currently serving time for either murder or manslaughter, 44% of those women had killed either their husband or intimate partner. However, of those women who had revealed that they had killed their spouse, 96% of them also admitted to having suffered domestic violence in the relationship.

Overwhelmingly, the reason that women kill is to escape a relationship with an abusive partner. With this knowledge, the next question is: what of the women who kill without the thought of self-defense in mind? What are the reasons and motives of the women who kill their perfectly loving and agreeable spouses? The women who kill in self-defense can be empathized with. But there is still a seedy underside to female murderers, the ones who manipulate the people around them and use others to their advantage to do away with their spouses. Not all women kill directly, after all. Some women manipulate others to do the deed for them.

The story of Pamela Ann Smart began in 1967. She was born as Pamela Wojas, on August 6th, in Coral Gables, Florida. A middle child, Pamela grew up as the second of three children. Her sister, Elizabeth, was six years her senior while her brother, John, was three years her junior. The children were born to a father who worked as a commercial airline pilot and a mother who was a part-time legal secretary. Her home life was good, and she went through childhood unmarred by violence or abuse by either her siblings or her parents. During her elementary school days, Pamela and her family moved from Florida to Windham, New Hampshire. There, Pamela flourished. She attended high school at Pinkerton Academy in Derry. She became a cheerleader, and her high school days floated by, still untouched by any particular violence or trauma. She was popular, and while she had a strained relationship with her father, she was very close to her mother.

After high school, Pamela decided to return to Florida for college. She attended the Florida State University and during her time there, Pamela worked on the radio, where she hosted a once a week show at WVFS. The show had a theme of heavy metal music, which Pamela loved. She called the show "Metal Madness", and her radio personality was under the alias of "Maiden of Metal". Pamela had a love for both heavy metal music and radio. After all, she was getting her degree in communications. Combining these two loves seemed like the only logical choice. It was during her time in college that Pamela met Gregory Smart. The year was 1986, and they were both at a New Year's Eve party. Pamela and Greg hit it off right away. Their relationship was intense from the beginning, and the two were seriously connected by February of 1987.

In 1988, Pamela graduated with honors and a degree in communications. Pamela was a smart and studious woman. Her academic achievements were nothing to be looked down upon. She achieved her degree in just over 3 years at the Florida State University, while maintaining a 3.85 grade point average. A year after her graduation, in 1989, Pamela and Gregory finally married, and Pamela went from Wojas to Smart. The marriage began as most marriages do, with a honeymoon phase that lasted only a short while. But while it lasted, the two were absolutely devoted to one another. They settled down in their hometown of Derry in New Hampshire, with a beautiful home on a quiet, residential street. Greg even bought Pamela a Shih Tzu, which she named 'Halen' after her favorite heavy metal group, Van Halen. Married young, Pamela was only 23 and Greg was absolutely devoted to her. They were the all American couple. Greg was excited about the start of his new life, with his perfect wife. His family recalls him talking at length about how Pamela would become a wonderful mother, so certain of his new wife's caretaking abilities.

Pamela, perhaps, was not as eager to begin life as a mother. She often described herself as a "typical Leo". That is to say, she always desired to be the center of attention. She had always been popular, even in high school, and she carried that bubbling charisma with her everywhere she went. While she was outgoing, loud and boisterous in her personality, Pamela was also needed to be in control: of herself and her surroundings, including the people in them. Her clothes were always nearly coordinated by color, and she lived by a very strict schedule that didn't allow much room for disruption. When her self-imposed schedule was thrown off, Pamela would become upset.

Despite their fundamental differences, Pamela and Greg had a happy marriage - for a short time.

It was only 7 months into the marriage before the happiness the two shared started to waver. Their relationship went from blissful happiness to having serious issues. It's no surprise that the honeymoon phase of any relationship would begin to fade, but after only seven months Pamela and Greg's relationship was facing challenges. While Pamela longed to continue their rock and roll image, Greg began to grow up more quickly not long after their marriage. He cut his long blonde hair that Pamela had first fallen for, which was only the beginning of Greg's new, conservative attitude. He took up a job at the same company that his own father worked at. He traded in his intense love for heavy metal, which had first brought him and Pamela together, for the ambition that it took to become an accomplished salesman. Pamela and Greg were simply growing apart as people, perhaps having married each other at too young of an age.

It was nearing their first year anniversary when Greg finally admitted to Pamela that he was having an affair. From then on, Pamela admitted, that her trust had been broken. She didn't feel important to her husband anymore. Her own interest in the marriage began to wane. After the admittance of the affair, Pamela's interests had turned into her career. After all, the graduated early with an astounding grade point average. Her desire to pursue a broadcasting career had not diminished in the slightest. Greg was unaware that Pamela wanted out of the marriage after the problem with the affair arose. Although she brought it up during every argument, talk of separation never came up.

Pamela, with her unhappy marriage and desire for freedom, took up a job at Winnacunnet High School in Hampton, New Hampshire, as a communications director. While it wasn't the glamorous job in broadcasting that she was hoping for, Pamela believed that it was a step in the right direction. Her duties included producing and distributing educational videos to the school districts. It wasn't quite the same as her heyday as the Metal Mistress back in college, but she was granted both her own secretary and student intern. In addition to this, Pamela also volunteered at the local drug awareness program, Project Self-Esteem, as an adult facilitator. She made a big impression on the freshman who were expected to participate in the program. All of the freshman students at Winnacunnet High School enjoyed Pamela - she was young, pretty and she could relate to them through a shared interested in heavy metal music.

Pamela got along well with the freshman who participated in the program. She was never patronizing and was young enough that she and the kids shared a lot of the same vernacular. She even wowed them with stories of her time in the heavy metal scene and her wild times backstage at concerts.

It was at Project Self Esteem that Pamela Smart met Billy Flynn. Their ill-fated meeting would change the course of both of their lives for good.

William "Billy" Flynn and Pamela Smart met in the fall of 1989. He was 15 years old, and one of the teenagers that worked on Project Self-Esteem. He was smitten with her right from the beginning, and would often go out of his way to help her. He even made routine visits to her office after the meetings. Billy Flynn shared Pamela's love for rock music. He was attractive and still growing into his looks, with blonde hair down to his shoulders - the same hairstyle that Pamela had loved in her own husband, and lamented it's lost. Despite his age, Pamela wasn't much older than most of the kids that she spent her days around, and it was easy for her to get lost in their acceptance. Around the same time that Pamela and Billy met, she was also reeling from her husband's admitted affair.

It was no surprise that Billy Flynn got caught up with Pamela. He was born just one day after an explosive argument between his parents and was always caught in the middle of their rocky relationship. He grew up watching his father mistreat his mother through anger and overbearing control. As the first child, it wasn't long until Billy was also the subject of his father's anger, and continued to experience it even after his siblings were born. Billy's father was reportedly a great man when things were going his way, but once that stopped his anger got the best of him and he would start yelling and berating whoever was within earshot. This put a strain on Billy and his relationship with his father.

Finally, spurred by his father having an affair, Billy's parents divorced. Soon after, Billy and his brothers moved with their mother from California to New Hampshire. It was here that Billy, young, angry, and suffering the trauma of a divorce, would meet Pamela, and change the course of his entire life.

Pamela's affair with Billy Flynn began when he was just 15. Pamela had become overly friendly with another one of the students under her charge, Cecelia Pierce, who was the student intern assigned to her at her position as a communications director. Pamela and Cecelia were like best friends, and Pamela showered her with attention. Because of their age differences, Pamela most likely made Cecelia feel important. After all, she was only 15 and Pamela was 23, an interesting adult who wanted to hang out with her and treated her like an intimate friend. Pamela's friendship with Cecelia soon began to show signs of being controlling, just as her "Leo" personality would suggest. The more time she spent with Pamela, the more her grades began to slip.

Pamela, Cecelia, and Billy would hang out like teenagers. While Gregory was out of the house, Pamela would invite the two teens over to watch movies or work on video projects together. It was during one of these times that Pamela and Billy first engaged in sexual intercourse. The time of the year was near the end of March, and Pamela had invited both Cecelia and Billy over to watch movies while her husband was out of state for a business meeting. After one of the movies ended, Cecelia went outside to walk Halen, the beloved Shih Tzu. While she was gone, Pamela brought Billy up to her bedroom, where she put on a piece of lingerie that she had bought specifically to seduce Billy Flynn. It was there, while their friend was out walking the dog, that the two had sex for the first time, in Pamela and Gregory's marriage bed.

Despite all the things she and the teenagers had in common, it's hard to understand why a grown woman would choose a 15-year-old as her lover - unless, of course, Pamela had other plans in mind for the needy and impressionable Billy Flynn. The morning after their first time together, Pamela said to Billy: "Last night was great, but we can't keep on like that." When Billy questioned why, Pamela said, "Because of Greg. If you want to keep seeing me, you'll have to get rid of my husband."

And just like that, the seed of Pamela's plan was planted. All that was left was to help it grow into a murderous, poisonous plant. Despite her conviction that they couldn't keep seeing one another, Pamela continued to engage in her relationship with Billy over the course of the next few weeks. Each time, she would continue to complain about the looming threat that her husband posed to their budding relationship. She even confided in Billy that Greg would beat her—although, this wasn't true. She continued to threaten that they couldn't keep seeing one another unless her husband was gone. Pamela explained to Billy that she couldn't get a divorce because her husband was too controlling. She told the young man that she would lose the condo and her dog. Billy, who had no reason to distrust his friend, teacher, and lover, believed the lies that she fed him. He was hopelessly in love, and it was then that the plans began to solidify.

Billy Flynn agreed with kill Pamela's husband. She had manipulated this outcome by repeatedly holding her affection and relationship hostage from him, with Gregory Smart as the threat that would tear them apart. Billy Flynn, just 15 years old and without the constitution of a murderer, flaked out on two attempts at Gregory's life. Each time, Pamela would berate him, threatening to leave him. While Billy couldn't yet see it, Pamela's motivations were clear: she was using her position of authority and her sexuality to manipulate Billy Flynn into committing the murder that she so desperately longed to commit, but refused to risk getting caught for. There was no star-crossed love between them, an angry husband keeping them apart. Pamela knew that she could manipulate a lonely, starry-eyed boy into disposing of her husband, and it wouldn't matter what happened to him after that.

Billy Flynn, faced with the threat of being left by the woman that he considered his lover, knew that he would have to start thinking seriously about killing Gregory Smart. He would later tell the jury that he thought Pamela would leave him if he chickened out of the murder one more time. Billy started confiding in his two friends, J.R and Pete, who had been in Billy's circle since he moved to New Hampshire from California. The three boys began plotting, with Pamela as encouragement. She gave them a deadline of May 1st, and promised the boys a cut of the insurance money that she would later collect.

While the boys were planning their attempt on Gregory's life, Pamela and her husband's marriage was falling into further disarray. Of course, this would be no surprise. After all, Gregory was living with a woman who was actively planning to kill him. There was no love left between them, and the strains of the marriage continued. They fought often and argued over the pettiest things. Gregory would come home to an empty house, and the couple would not see each other for days on end. Regardless of Pamela's desire to see him dead, the marriage was clearly ending. The two young lovers had simply grown apart. Where Gregory had grown into a businessman with responsibilities, Pamela had decided to stay surrounded by teenagers and relive her youth a while longer.

Finally, the plan to dispose of Gregory Smart was coming together. Unsurprising to anyone, it was Pamela who gave the boys primary directions. Pamela would leave her backdoor and cellar open. Billy, J.R, and Pete would enter the house and begin to tear it apart, making it look as if a robbery had taken place. She even instructed them to take electronics, jewelry and anything valuable to make it seem real. The lights were to stay off, as Pamela insisted that if her husband saw any of the lights on, he wouldn't come inside. She also didn't want the dog to be hurt, and so she instructed the boys to stick Halen in the basement so he wouldn't be traumatized by witnessing the murder of one of his owners. Finally, Pam insisted that they use a knife rather than a gun because she didn't want blood all over the apartment.

The plan would conclude with Pamela coming home to discover her husband, ostensibly murdered during a vicious robbery attempt.

May 1st, 1990, was the day that the plan would take place. That morning, Pamela got up and acted as if it were any other day and not the very last day of her husband's life. She exchanged morning pleasantries with her husband as they went about their morning routines. She tended to Halen and the two had breakfast together before they parted ways. Pamela must have been hyper aware of what was going on, and what would happen, while she watched her husband go about his day without any knowledge that it was his last. After all, most people never know which day is their last.

Gregory left for work before Pamela, who then headed out the door around 9:45 that morning. She had plans that would keep her busy all day and give her the alibi she needed to get away with conducting and orchestrating her husband's murder. She was attending a school board meeting that planned to go later than usual due to a salary review. Attending this meeting would ensure that Pamela wouldn't return home until after night had fallen - until Gregory was dead. Around 2:30 in the afternoon, Pamela and Billy met by his locker to discuss a small hiccup in their plan: they needed a ride to go pick up the getaway car, which belonged to J.R's grandmother. Perhaps leaving three teenage boys to do the dirty work is dispatching her husband wasn't the smartest idea that Pamela had, but it was all she had to work with. All the same, Pamela drove one of the boys out to get the car, and the rest of the plan was back in action.

Just before 8:30 pm, Billy, J.R, Pete and a fourth boy, named Raymond Fowler, commenced with the plan. Raymond was a boy often on the periphery of the group. His role in the plan was minor. Billy and Pete entered the condo while the other boys waited outside in the courtyard. While the ransacked the house, Billy tossed Halen into the basement - the dog, reportedly, fell down the stairs while the other boys laughed. After the dog was locked downstairs, they continued on with the plan that Pamela had set out for them. They took jewelry and took apart the electronics to make it look like a real robbery. After they had done their duty messing up the condo, Billy Flynn and Pete waited in the darkness for Gregory Smart to return home from his day, entirely unaware that they would be waiting for him.

Despite Pamela's insistence that they use a knife because of the mess, J.R had taken a gun from his father's collection and given it to Billy. The boys waited in the darkness by the backdoor, ready to jump Gregory the moment that he entered. When he did, it was Billy who leaped first, out of the darkness and onto Gregory. Pamela's husband was immediately overtaken by Billy and Pete. They stole his wedding ring to complete the robbery-gone-wrong image.

Finally, Billy said: "God forgive me," as he pulled the trigger just inches from Gregory Smart's head, and the man dropped dead to the floor.

The plan was completed. The boys escaped the condo, and their friends were waiting with the getaway car. They made their way back home. Billy had completed the task that Pamela had set out for him to do. He had killed her husband, in the anticipation that they would finally be able to be together. In the aftermath that followed, it was Pamela's job to play the grieving widow. According to the detective who worked on the case, Daniel Pelletier, she wasn't as good of an actress as she thought. Her interview with Detective Pelletier raised all kinds of concerns. Pelletier said, "From day one, she wasn't acting the grieving widow." Unfortunately, that was her only job in the plan she had concocted.

It was Pamela who insisted on an interview with the detective, and during that time Pelletier continued noticing strange things about her story. She described stepping over the body and noticing the speakers on the stand. She described the scene as a "botched robbery", rather than focusing on the death of her husband. The final thing that tipped Pelletier off, however, was when he took Pamela back to the condo to gather things she needed before closing it off as a crime scene: Pamela walked over the blood stain where her husband had died. Not around it: over it, multiple times until it was covered with a towel.

On May 2nd, just a day after the murder, detectives were already discussing the idea that it was Pamela who had done it, not yet aware of her influence on four teenage boys. It took two weeks before an anonymous tip led the detectives in the right direction: Cecelia Pierce. Detectives also got information from a boy named Ralph Welch, who had overheard J.R and Pete discussing their roles the homicide. While the detectives couldn't get the boys to talk, Cecelia finally told them everything. She agreed to be wired and tape a conversation between herself and Pamela in order to get the evidence that they needed. Pamela was convinced that it was her word against the boys and that she was home free, despite that word was getting around about her own involvement. It was Cecelia who managed to get Pamela's confession on tape, acknowledging that she knew that the murder was set to take place before it happened. That was all the police needed to set the rest of their plan into action to put Pamela away for good.

On August 1st, 1990, Pelletier arrested Pamela Smart for first-degree murder. Police Captain Jackson was on the scene as well, and had this to say of Pamela: "She thought she was smart, but she had no street smarts. [...] That was the problem. She that she was smarter than the whole world. But she made many mistakes, right and left."

The trial lasted only 14 days, and the main argument was about whether or not Pamela Smart had control of Billy Flynn and the other boys enough to make them murder her husband, or whether those boys did it on their own. Pamela continually insisted that she had no prior knowledge, and that she had lied to Cecelia on the tapes received of their phone calls. Pamela admitted to the affair with Billy Flynn, but refused to admit to prior knowledge of the planned murder. Her testimony consisted of confessions of love for the teenager. When it was Billy Flynn's turn to take the stand, he described everything: from Pamela's insistence that he kill her husband, to the night of the murder.

"I cocked the hammer back and pointed the gun at his head. I stood there for a hundred years, it seemed like," Billy Flynn said in his testimony. And while the court argued back and forth whether or not Pamela had controlled Billy to do what he had done, it was clear why he had done it.

On March 22nd, 1991, the jury deliberated for all of 13 hours before they came back with a verdict: guilty. Pamela was sentenced to life without parole on the charge of accomplice to first-degree murder. A follow-up hearing sentences her with conspiracy to commit first-degree murder and witness tampering. New York State, where she still remains to this day serving her life sentence.

As for the boys, Billy Flynn and Pete are serving their time at the Maine State Prison in Warren, Maine. The fourth boy, Raymond Fowler, was paroled in 2003, sent back after violating the terms, but released again in 2005. J.R was given a 30-year sentence that was then reduced by 12 years to 18, and he was paroled in 2005. Cecelia Pierce, on the other hand, came out on top, having signed away the rights to her story of the case for $100,000.

Pamela Smart is an interesting case when it comes to women who kill. After all, she didn't lay a hand on her husband. However, she abused the influence that she had on her impressionable students and managed to use a combination of sex and power and to manipulate a young boy into committing a crime that he could never take back, and one that would never have crossed his mind had Pamela not been the one to put it there. So, despite the fact that she wasn't even in the house while her husband was killed, Pamela Smart still goes down in history as one of the most infamous "women who kill".

AMNESIAC KILLER : THE TRUE STORY OF DANIELLE STEWART

85

LES ACKERMAN

"I would punish all of those who had never lost anything, those who had never had anything taken away from them. I would let the anger from my chest reach out and explode in spectacular violence." - An excerpt from a poem by Danielle Stewart

Danielle Stewart had a normal and happy childhood until around the age of seven. Both of her parents were public servants and the family lived in the Curtin, Canberra region of Australia. She had one younger sister and the family seemed en route to living a normal, happy life.

Danielle was particularly close to her father during her childhood years. He took her swimming, read books to her at night and sang to her. She described him as being a man with a great sense of humor and the kind of man who "did all the things that dads do."

At the age of seven, however, Danielle's life took a traumatic turn. Her family was building a holiday house in the NSW south coast town of Batemans Bay. Danielle, unfortunately, came into the cross hairs of a sexual predator.

The man was a neighbor and Danielle would come over to his home to watch TV as they had no television of their own in their holiday house. The man was a married real estate agent in his 50s. He would let Danielle and a friend come with him to outings where they would examine unoccupied houses he was selling. It was there, inside these homes, that the assaults would take place.

Danielle would be under the man's spell for over three years before they molestations came to an end.

When she was eleven years old, tragedy struck again in the form of losing her mother to cancer. Distraught, her father sent her away for a weekend with a friend of a family. The family had a teenaged son, however, who constantly harassed Danielle, molesting her as well.

Her father would remarry six months later to a woman who had three children of her own. Danielle felt betrayed by her father's remarriage and tried to commit suicide with an overdose of pills. Her father himself had suffered from depression and fell apart emotionally after the death of Danielle's mother.

"I've always believed that depression and mental illness is inheritable," forensic psychologist Pauline Malloy said. "Sometimes through genetics, sometimes through thought processes. With Danielle, she clearly inherited some mental illness from her father's side of the family as her dad suffered from depression as well as her paternal grandfather."

Her maternal grandparents arrived and offered that Danielle come live with them. Danielle didn't want to go, she wanted to stay with her Dad but her father didn't want her screwing up the dynamics of his new family with her bad behavior.

He wanted her gone.

So Danielle was given two choices, either go live with her grandparents or go to a youth shelter.

Danielle chose to run away

"Danielle suffered numerous traumas, back to back," Malloy said. "The loss of her innocence, the loss of her mom and then the rejection of her father. Any of the above could have been cause for life altering psychological trauma but she suffered all of these within a four year time span. It had to crush her psychically and she did not have the life experience to cope."

Running away, the twelve year old girl roughed it out on the streets. Finally, she grew tired and returned home to her father. She would not be treated as the prodigal daughter, however, as her father had her bags packed and waiting. He drove Danielle to a local youth shelter and dropped her off.

Danielle would remain there for the next three months.

Danielle did not like the youth refuge. There was a lot of drug use, alcohol and she once again experienced sexual abuse.

"This was a horrid life for her at this point," Malloy said. "At some point I think she broke down psychologically and the seeds for future violent behavior were planted here."

RETURNING HOME

She eventually returned home to live with her father but he had settled in with his new family.

"I felt so alone, unloved, misunderstood," Danielle recalled. "and as the problems at home got worse, I got worse. I was sneaking out of the house, drinking, drugging. I missed my mum so terribly, I just wanted to be with her."

Danielle would attempt suicide on several occasions, leaving permanent scars on her wrist.

"I used a razor in my bedroom downstairs," Danielle said. "There was no internet back then and I didn't know how to do it [properly]."

On her 13th birthday, her father celebrated by throwing her out of the house once again. She would go and live with her friend Elle O'Brien and her mother. O'Brien's mother fed her and took her in, allowing the unwanted girl to remain there for four years.

At the age of sixteen, she enrolled at Narrabundah College and become a student of renowned poet Geoff Page.

"She was leagues ahead of anyone I've encountered writing contemporary poetry at that age," Page recalled. "She had some of the same virtues as Sylvia Plath, a real feeling for adventurous imagery. There was a lot going on in her brain at an intense level and she had the talent to turn it into something moving."

Under the guidance of her teacher, Danielle published an anthology of poems called "I for Icarus."

Danielle would go on to study performing arts at Melbourne's Monash University before traveling to Sydney to share an apartment with her step-sister, Myfanwy Thompson. Both young women would indulge in alcohol and prescription drugs, becoming the catalyst for each others self-destructive behavior. Myfanwy, however, would suffer a freak accident in falling off a cliff while taking ecstasy.

The loss devastated Danielle as she considered Myfanwy to be her best friend.

"Her boyfriend had got into dealing ecstasy," Danielle said. "I couldn't handle seeing her wasted all the time, so I'd moved out with other friends."

Her younger step-brother, Tristram would later die of an aneurysm after being diagnosed with schizophrenia.

MEANDERING THROUGH LIFE

Danielle was now 24 and wandered aimlessly through life. She went from one job to the next until she met the 50-year old Chaim Kimel in late 2000.

"They met on the dance floor and hit it off immediately," journalist Byron Kaye said.

Despite the age difference, Chaim Kamel was a stylish man with his own business.

"He was a bit of a bon vivant," crime author Paul Kidd said. "Lived in the good part of Sydney. A good lifestyle."

"He was very charismatic, very gregarious, very charming, very generous, strong and creative," Danielle said. "He loved his children and they loved him."

Kimel had been a successful entrepreneur, dealing in antiques. She got a job working for Chaim in his furniture store, Eclectica in Mosman. Kimel had put Danielle in charge of bookkeeping.

The two got along exceptionally well, at first, with common interests in art, music, and food.

"Danielle was a very attractive," Kidd said. "Petite, blonde, loved to drink. He (Chaim) was an older man but a really good style of a bloke."

The relationship started platonic in the beginning.

"He made some advances which weren't initially reciprocated," Kaye said. "But over time, they became intimate and it was on."

Kimel thought Danielle was a "prize catch". He invited Danielle over to visit his family and she was impressed with how close and living they were. There she saw, for the first time since her early childhood, a loving family that she could be a part of.

Danielle moved in with Kimel who had the time lived with his ten year old son Jordan. He also had a daughter, Amber and Fred, who were in their early twenties and late teens respectively.

A CHANGE IN DEMEANOR?

One of her friends, however, thought that Danielle changed after she met Chaim. She described him as being very possessive and told her what to do.

"I loved him," Danielle said. "I still do. It is a love-hate thing and it won't ever go. With those types of personalities, there is that level of attention, you become their entire focus."

Danielle would have these kind of intense relationships all of her life and it seemed to be the fuel to her fire. She was irresistibly drawn to the drama and would have it on full blast with Chaim Kimel.

"Anyone who would have been in a relationship with Danielle Stewart would have been in a relationship that was doomed from the start," Kidd said. "The combination of psychological problems fueled by excesses of alcohol was always going to end in disaster."

COCAINE AND BOOZE

Danielle began substance abuse at an early age which only progressed as she got older. She now had a benefactor in Chaim as well as an enabler as he liked to party, indulging in cocaine himself.. He didn't realize, however, that the alcohol would only stoke the flames that would extinguish their relationship.

He also had a dark side, according to Danielle's grandmother. She described him as someone who was "demanding and overpowering."

"She (Danielle) went through life with a paranoia that people were going to leave her," Kidd said. "And she became very, very possessive of her partner and that fueled by alcohol was the basis of the majority of their problems."

CALL THE POLICE

Once the relationship turned intimate, things started getting out of hand. The two indulged in alcohol and had numerous fights in which the police were called in.

Danielle had been taking strong anti-depression medications and mixing these drugs with alcohol. One fight had gotten so severe that she took a restraining order out against Kimel.

On one occasion, Kimel violated the order and was jailed for one night.

"I'd moved into temporary accommodation and Chaim came after me," Danielle said. "He broke into my room and stole my laptop and wallet. The police busted him on the way out and took him to jail for the night."

Kimel explained to the police that he violated the order because Danielle had called him stating that she had swallowed fourteen Valiums.

"I'm fine when I'm not in an emotional situation," Danielle said, "but when I'm under threat, the flashbacks can be extreme."

"She (Danielle) had a borderline personality disorder," Malloy said. "When things go bad with her, they go real bad. That was how she lived her entire life up until that point. She had to engage in fights, drinking, drugs. Drama, drama, drama. If it isn't there, she will create it."

A PROPENSITY FOR VIOLENCE

Kimel's son, Jordan, was ten years old when his father first met Danielle. He recalled Danielle as a destructive psychotic stating that she would "cut up $10,000 worth of business suits, delete important documents from my father's computer. Once, she punched through a glass bathroom window and slashed her wrists. And she'd punch my father, too."

"Unfortunately, this was the pattern that was set," Malloy set. "They would argue, fight and then get back together. When they would get back together things would be more passionate and clingy than before. 'Please, don't leave me,' that sort of thing. But then the cycle repeats itself and it has to be more extreme in order for the couple to get that same 'high.'"

The couple would remain together and make attempts to appear respectable. In 2004, Danielle enrolled at a nearby college to finish her degree while they both started an online catering company called Epicurean. The money to start the company was borrowed from Danielle's grandmother, a total of $30,000.

Later that year, the couple would journey to India where they would marry at the Taj Mahal.

Danielle would claim, however, that the money the borrowed for the business is what kept her in the marriage .

"Part of the reason I married Chaim was because I was worried about my grandparents' money," Danielle said. "If I left him, there'd be no legal recourse for me to get it back. He took it without shame; he never planned to pay it back."

"Typical of people with borderline personality disorders," Malloy said. "Is that they have to play the role of the victim. It is a head scratcher as to why Chaim would borrow thirty-grand when he had his own business. Maybe he thought he would be placating her somehow with them being in business together and having her feel as if she were a part of things. But clearly he didn't need anything more on his plate."

BOOMERANG BABY

Danielle would leave Kimel a total of seven times during their seven year relationship. She would confide in her grandmother and friend Elle, saying she was unhappy. Then he would call and they would get back together.

"It (their relationship) was very alcohol fueled," Kaye said. "Very hedonistic. A lot of violent arguments."

Danielle blamed her inability to stay away from Chaim on her lack of self-esteem.

"While he could be caring, it was undermined by his desire to keep me enslaved to him," Danielle said. "When I left him, he'd follow me and get me back. When your sense of self-esteem is so low and a learnt helplessness has set in, you don't feel able to support yourself. My friends had dropped off because they couldn't stand him. The only times I responded with violence were when I was trying to leave and he'd try to stop me. He'd hide my wallet, phone, computer, passport. Those times always ended with me being in hospital, not him. I never tried to kill him: I tried to kill myself."

WHO WAS ABUSING WHO?

It became apparent to Kimel's family, however, that he had married a woman prone to violent outbursts. Kimel told his daughter than Danielle had bitten him on his thumb and arm as as smashing his glasses.

He had his glasses broken so much that it had become a "running joke", according to his daughter Amber.

After arguments, Danielle would delete Kimel's emails and computer files. Kimel had became so enraged at her actions that he kicked her out of the house. Danielle would return, kicking out the timber door.

WELCOME TO THE PSYCH WARD

Danielle had overdosed on medication numerous times during the course of her marriage. She would inform doctors that Kimel was controlling and that she had "nothing to live for."

His daughter, Amber, however, expressed concern for her father's well being and wanted him to sever ties with Danielle.

"He told me he'd made a commitment to be there for her and loved her unconditionally," Amber said. "He was convinced unconditional love would cure her."

"Chaim was the rescuer," Malloy said. "He couldn't help himself. Danielle was the beautiful damsel in distress. They had passionate sex together, he knew about her past, and he couldn't be another man that brought more pain in her life. He didn't want that. He thought that through his own sincerity and love that he could somehow bring her to a place of healing. But he wasn't a professional. And that isn't what relationships are for."

A NEW MAN

In 2006, Danielle separated from Kimel and met Melbourne university professor Joeri Mol. She moved in with him and became pregnant by December of that year. Danielle wanted to go back to Sydney, however, and didn't want to raise the child with Mol as a single mother.

"She went out with somebody else," Kaye said. "He was seeing other people but they could not stop speaking. They remained extremely close. The new fellow (Mol) wants to settle down and start raising a family. Which incidentally was Danielle's greatest dream, which was to have a family. But she's still drawn to Chaim uncontrollably."

A week later, she called Kimel and the two met to discuss a reconciliation.

"He (Chaim) told her that either she as a termination," Kidd said. "Or there's no hope if them ever getting back together."

She complied with his request, her second abortion in six months (the first with Kimel) and she once again went into a depression.

"Danielle desperately wanted to experience the happiness that she had before her mother died," Malloy said. "She always told her grandmother, 'I just want have a normal life. I just want to have a normal life.' What she really wanted was that family again. So now she spends her life grasping at straws, going from this man to that man, and getting multiple abortions."

BURNING THE CANDLE AT BOTH ENDS

The couple moved back in together in 2007 but this time their break-up would be much more volatile.

And violent.

"It was short lived (their reconciliation)," Kidd said. "Now that they were back together. It was business as usual."

Business as usual was a lot of fighting and alcohol coupled with a flurry of activity to keep up with the bills.

Danielle returned to college and continued to run their catering business, The Epicurean. In order to make ends meet, however, she took a part time job at a Sydney ad agency.

She couldn't juggle all of these things at once, so she turned to cocaine and alcohol. Her friends described her as "withdrawn" and "unsettled" after meeting with her after the latest reconciliation.

Danielle began to feel the itch to run away again, telling friends she now just wanted to earn some money on her own and get away from Kimel for good.

"How the hell could this have worked to begin with?" Malloy said. "You've got a woman with some serious issues, abused by men, abandoned as a child and now she's an alcoholic with major depression. The pattern is set in their relationship. Break-up, get back together, fight some more. Rinse and repeat. This can only end badly. The question was, how bad?"

THE FATEFUL DINNER

"The old problems kept resurfacing," Kaye said. "They kept on with the dinner parties. Living the good life. And with this came Danielle's terrible response to alcohol access."

On August 23rd of 2007, Danielle went out with Kimel to have dinner at a restaurant called Pescador. They were described in a police statement by their friend, Angela Batley, to be in "good spirits."

"It is noted by others there that Danielle seemed a little drunker than usual," Kaye said. "Things got a little bit more testy and Danielle left and decided to walk home."

After dinner, Chaim went with his friends to Angela Batley's home. He would call Danielle from the home and she said that she would come and pick him up. Things took a turn for the strange when Danielle came over but drove back without Chaim who ended up walking home.

Batley was concerned about the tenseness of the situation and called Kimel to make sure he got home safe. Kimel told Batley that Danielle was working on the computer but was "drunk" and that he had to go.

Danielle arrived at their home before Kimel. She told the 16-year old Jordan that she "shouldn't have gone to Angela's house. I've had too much to drink."

Jordan stated that Danielle began playing loud music through the computer, dancing with a drink in her hand. When Kimel arrived, he told her to turn the music down before the neighbors start complaining. An argument ensued before Kimel turned off Danielle's music himself. The argument escalated, the topics being the loud music then escalating to the fact that Chaim would change the password on the computer, which was an ongoing issue in their relationship.

She started to physically attack him but Chaim easily evaded the rushes of the drunk Danielle. Then in the heat of the moment, she picked up one of Chaim's antique ornamental knives he had on display. Chaim came forward, ordering her to place the knife down, then she stuck it into his stomach.

Chaim fell to the ground and she stabbed him again.

"They were both yelling for about 15 minutes," stated Jordan. "All of a sudden, I could hear them in the corridor outside my room. It sounded like someone was being hit or punched and I heard my father say, 'Why are you being violent and attacking me?' They kept fighting and I heard Danielle fall to the floor and scream. Soon after this, I heard my father say in a tense voice, 'What are you doing? Are you crazy?' I heard my father scream three times. I saw [his] white shirt was covered in blood all up the left side from underneath his ribs towards the middle of his torso. Danielle was standing about two metres away and she had our antique knife in her hand."

Jordan saw his father struggling to get to the front door. He was covered in blood and Danielle was hysterical, holding up the knife.

"So the son runs out of his room," Kaye said. "He finds his father clutching his stomach where he's been stabbed twice. Covered in blood. Barely able to speak."

Jordan then thought about attacking Danielle himself.

"He picks up a golf club then thinks for a moment, that he might avenge his father," Kaye said. "It's actually Chaim himself who tells him don't do it. Lying there, sort of holding himself together. The son puts the golf club down and nurses his father while he lies there dying."

Kimel would be rushed to the hospital but die on the operating table at St. Vincent's Hospital, bleeding to death from the two stab wounds to his stomach.

"To the end of his life," Malloy said. "Kimel was protecting Danielle. When his son wanted revenge, he held him back."

Danielle was arrested but plead not guilty on the grounds of self defense. Her blood alcohol reading, however, was five times the legal driving limit.

"It was a stupid, pointless, uncontrolled lover's argument," Kaye said. "And one split second decision led to this terrible outcome."

Danielle maintained no recollection of the events, as she mixed the anti-psychotic drug Seroquel with alcohol. She awoke in a prison cell and called out for her husband, seeing her name on the board with the word 'Murder' written next to it.

"It was the worst moment of my life," Danielle recalled. "In one instant, my entire life had changed and Chaim's had ended."

"Something was going to happen that night," Malloy said. "Her mind was on edge. This may not have been pre-meditated but she knew what was going to happen when she picked up that knife. Remember, she didn't just slash at him as a warning. She thrust the knife into Chaim. Not once. But twice. There was an untapped rage there that came to the surface at the moment. It had been bubbling for a long, long time and unfortunately Chaim Kimel could not foresee how this would end."

THE AFTERMATH

Danielle made a recorded phone call to her father a few days after the killing.

"If I could swap Chaim with me right now, I would do it immediately," Danielle said. "There is no way I meant to kill him."

"Again, I don't think the murder was pre-planned," Malloy said. "But it did seem to be part of Danielle's destiny. What we see here in her killing of Chaim was a metaphor of her own trauma. She was abused by a man in his fifties, molested by him from the ages of seven through ten. She grows into a beautiful woman can choose just about whatever man she wants but instead she elects a man in his fifties, over twenty-five years her senior. That is no coincidence. She is repeating her trauma from the past. But this time she wants to control it. She wants to exorcise the demons of the past so all of those violent fights are trial runs until finally she reaches for that knife and stabs Chaim, metaphorically killing the molester of her past. Now her husband, who actually really loved her, is the victim of this cycle of abuse that has finally come full circle."

Her father agreed to post Danielle's bail but would not agree to the 24-hour surveillance condition attached to it. Her father abandoning her yet again, she turned to her friend Elle O'Brien's mother. She came to bail out Danielle and secured her release after nine months.

Danielle then went to live with her grandmother.

Facing twenty-five years in prison, Danielle would attempt suicide two more times, one of them involving an overdose of Seroquel.

"When I took that Seroquel, I went into psychosis," Danielle said. "It was an out-of-body experience where I thought the nurses were talking about me even though they weren't. I was watching myself from afar. It was crazy, crazy shit. I am sure that is what must have happened on the night Chaim died."

"The psych med plus alcohol defense has become a cliched defense for a lot of killers," Malloy said. "Danielle had done her research. She had studied scriptwriting in school. Everything she said and did had a rehearsed feel to it."

FROM MURDER TO MANSLAUGHTER

The murder charge had been downgraded to manslaughter as Danielle maintained she had no recollection of what happened. She did not remember any of the events of what happened that night not to mention taking the ornamental knife and stabbing her husband with it.

She did not take the stand, however.

"Danielle was charged with murder," Kaye said. "She wept throughout much of the trial. It was very clear that she regretted what she'd done and she wanted him back and she felt quite horrible."

Kimel's children, however, saw Danielle as an imposter the more they investigated the case. They found a synopsis of a play that Danielle had been working on. In the story, one of the characters had a secret desire to kill her older husband.

Fred Kimel, Chaim's oldest son, noted that the play contained details on "jail architecture, prisoner psychology, different cell classifications, prisoner attire, prison visiting hours and life sentences."

The Kimel family once enamored with Danielle, now saw her in a completely different light.

"It was a university assignment, a book I was writing," Danielle said. "I heard that somewhere men kill their partners because they want them to stay, whereas women kill their partners because they want to escape. I know why I was writing about prison: because I was imprisoned long before I was [actually] incarcerated."

SENTENCING

Danielle would be sentenced to six years in prison. She would serve only four.

"There's no doubt that jail saved me," Danielle said. "It prevented me from harming myself with alcohol and drugs. I wouldn't recommend it, though."

During the first nine months of her term, she had been housed in the mental health unit. She could not stop crying. But the prison assigned her to a job in the kitchen and she found her fellow inmates to be helpful.

"I managed to get a few of the heavies on side somehow and avoided the others where possible," Danielle said. "I learnt to assimilate, to hide the fact that I was pretty and educated. I adapted where I could. In jail, I lost everything that made me me: my family, dog, business, house, studies, friends, freedom, clothes, make-up, choices. All I had was myself, my mind and my heart. I learnt to spot evil from a mile away - and evil does exist, I've come face to face with it - but I could still love. This is how I got through jail. Yes, I learnt how to operate within the system, but I could still see beauty in people, and I tried to speak to that."

"Danielle was a well-spoken, educated young woman," Malloy said. "But why the hell would she plead not guilty? She did her research on prison culture beforehand so a cynic can argue that she got off very, very light for what she did. Call it misandry, call it getting the female pass, Danielle was able to get off light for a cold-blooded murderer. She used all of the things from her past to mitigate her own culpability. Sexual abuse, parental death and abandonment down to psych meds and alcohol. She combined those things to get sympathy from Chaim and later from the her jury of her crime."

Danielle walked out of prison on June 24th, 2010.

She is now focused on the prospect of moving to Spain and becoming a professional writer.

"I've paid for what has happened and I've done all I can to fix the issues within myself that contributed to Chaim's death," Danielle said. "I see both a psychiatrist and a psychologist, both of my own volition, nothing to do with parole directives. I don't drink. I don't take drugs. I take responsibility for my actions. I write when I can. I try to love my friends and family. I try to see beauty in the world and I'd like to hope, one day, that I can contribute to that beauty. Still, I love. I still love Chaim. I still love my father. In the end, love will be all I have."

SHE KILLED THE PREACHER

John Fontaine

The Case of Mary Winkler

Mary Winkler, at first appearances, would seem to be an altogether normal woman. So too did her family, with a husband who was a Church minister and three young children, girls aged just eight, six and one.

The family lived in Selmer, Tenn., a small town occupied by around 4,500 people, according to the 2015 census. The town is situated to the south west of the state. Not much has happened in Selmer; the most famous person to have been born there was Chad Harville, former pitcher for the Oakland A's, and for one year, the Red Sox. He achieved a 4-9 win-loss record over his career in the MLB.

Today, the most famous- or infamous- person to have come from Selmer is Mary Winkler. In 2006, Mary sparked a border-crossing manhunt, and a court case followed nationwide. She had killed her husband with a shot to the back from the family's shotgun. But it was the gripping, and at times bizarre, court case which gripped the attention of the nation.

Matthew dead, Mary and the family Missing

The date was March 6th, 2007. It was a Tuesday like any other. Mary and Matthew were at home all day together, although Matthew was due to give a sermon that evening.

It was actually members of Matthew's congregation who found his body that night. They had visited his home to check up on him after he had missed the service he was set to give; instead, they found him lying dead, having been shot in the back.

There was no sign of Mary or any of their children at the home, and as such, they were reported missing. The authorities quickly sent out an Amber Alert, since nobody had any idea what could have happened to them, or where they might be. Family and friends had no information to provide police on their whereabouts.

There was every chance that the family had been kidnapped or murdered, and their bodies disposed of elsewhere, although police could not identify a break in, and had no reason to believe that anything of value had been stolen.

It was only a day later that she was arrested in Alabama, having run from the family home with her young children. They were found 350 miles away from home, at Orange Beach, and in the back seat of the van was the family's shotgun. It was certainly suspicious; but what reason could Mary have possibly had for committing such a crime?

The Trial

In the build up to the case going to trial, public interest ramped up. Speculation had been rife about why Mary would have murdered her husband, a seemingly nice, well respected member of the local community. Perhaps either one of them had had an affair, and Matthew had been killed in a crime of passion. Or maybe he had been killed for an insurance claim?

As such, the press reported every step of the story as it came out during the hearing. The trial began when a Tennessee Bureau of Investigation Agent John Mehr read a statement that Mary had made very soon after her arrest. In it, Mary claimed that the couple had been arguing about their family finances, before Mary had shot her husband with their 12 gauge shotgun. She had said that the last thing she had wanted was to actually murder her husband, but she had been brandishing the gun in an effort to convince him to work through their problems, together. The argument had been ongoing throughout the day, and Mary had finally snapped, resorting to drastic measures to be able to convince him. She had never intended to kill him: she had said in the statement, 'I don't want this at all. I don't want any of this to be, at all.'

The statement continued on, and Mary claimed that they had argued often and argued fiercely. 'He had really been on me lately,' Mary had said, 'criticizing me for things- the way I walk, I eat, everything. It was just building up to a point. I was tired of it. I guess I got to a point and snapped.'

At first glance, it would seem that Mary had simply lost her composure, become angry, and killed her husband 'as the red mist had descended'. But after their initial statement, Mary's attorney indicated that there was much more that would come out about Matthew's behaviour when she testified which would help to explain her actions. Clearly, there were more problems with their marriage than the occasional, albeit fierce, argument.

Mary's Crime

The case for the prosecution wasted no time in painting Mary as a cold blooded killer, who left her husband to die without remorse. Admittedly, the plain facts of the case made Mary seem unbelievably guilty. The prosecution relied on several of these facts in their attempt to convince the jury of Mary's guilt for the charge of murder.

Mary had disconnected the phone immediately after she shot her husband, stopping him from being able to call the emergency services, or receive any calls that may have come in. This suggested that Mary had been in full control of her actions, not panicking, since it is unlikely that somebody in a state of anxiety would think to disconnect the phone.

The fact that Mary had attempted to flee to Orange Beach, Alabama, was also a key point for the prosecution. Immediately after Matthew's death, Mary had taken the family minivan to the beach, with her three children. Later on in her defence, Mary would claim that she ran because '[n]obody would believe me, and they'd take the girls away and put me away.' Certainly, in many murder cases, the fact that the defendant flees the scene is a certain indicator of guilt.

The family's daughter Patricia testified that she couldn't understand her mother's actions. All that she knew was that she had heard a 'big boom', and the sound of something heavy hitting the floor. She quickly ran to the bedroom to see her father on the floor, and her mother holding the shotgun. She had no idea what could possibly have provoked her mother to shoot him.

Another sticking point was that the family finances had been 'in shambles' just before the murder had taken place. This had led Mary to become embroiled in what is called a 'check kiting' scam. In it, she had received checks from unidentified accounts in Canada and Nigeria, and had ultimately fallen to a financial scam that had lost the family money. Prosecutors claimed that this could have somehow instigated the argument that led to Matthew's death, and that Mary had felt as if she had no way out of the scam.

They also jumped on the fact that in an initial conversation with investigators, Mary had told them that their marriage was a happy one, and that '[t]here's no poor me. I'm in control.' They clearly wanted to paint a picture of Mary as remorseless, deceitful, and smarter than she looked.

The Cross-examination

During her cross-examination in court, Mary stated that she didn't remember grabbing the gun from the closet in which it was kept. What she did remember was that 'something went off', 'hearing a loud boom', and that 'it wasn't as loud as I thought it would be.' She did admit that she had shot her husband. Matthew rolled from the bed- upon which he had been lying as they had argued- and dropped to the floor. Mary described smelling gunpowder.

Prosecutor Walter Freeland asked her whether she understood that 'pulling a trigger is what makes it go boom', to which she replied that she did.

Matthew asked her why she had snapped and shot him. She could only say 'I'm sorry.' The shotgun blast had been inflicted from behind, directly into Matthew's back, and had caused severe damage to his organs and spine. According to prosecutors, he had in fact still been alive as Mary had run from the house.

But these simple facts were far from the end of the story, as Mary was to reveal.

Appearances and Revelations

At first, Mary spoke of her husband not in the past tense, but in the present, as if she couldn't quite understand how final her actions really had been. In reminiscing about happier times, Mary told the court that her husband was an intelligent, social man, and that the family had shared many 'good times' together. She also seemed to enjoy talking about her children, and the happiness they brought her.

This happy family life, however, was simply one side of the marriage. Mary's attorney stated that '[w]hat went on behind their closed doors is going to have to be told ... Some of what we've got from the state of Tennessee touches on sexual abuse.' Their defence was that Matthew had made Mary's life a 'living hell': '[w]e will show you proof that he would destroy objects that she loved, he would isolate her from her family and he would abuse her not just verbally, not just emotional and not just physically—in other ways, too.'

Just before the murder, Mary claimed that Matthew had been threatening their children and even attempted to throttle their infant daughter, Breanna. He had been shouting, angry, because he had wanted a son. As the case went on, it became obvious that this was only the tip of the iceberg, however, and more and more sordid details of their home life would come to light.

Matthew, Mary claimed, was a violent, abusive husband. Shortly after their marriage, he ordered her to stop socialising with any of her family and friends (a common tactic among abusive spouses in order to further isolate their partners from potential help). Winkler's sisters described how Mary seemed stuck in her marriage, unhappy, but unable to leave. In an interview, they said that 'As the years went on, she seemed to be nervous to show love towards us.'

Mary was commonly 'screamed and hollered' at by her husband. 'He just flailed. He's a big guy and he was just all over ... He'd point his finger inches away from my nose. Whatever he was upset about, it was my fault,' Mary had said. It could be over anything: 'I was fat, my hair wasn't right, the girls, if something went wrong, it was my fault. I didn't know when it was coming.' Mary described her situation as one familiar to abused wives and husbands across America.

Her attorney, Steve Farese, provided further information based on his conversations with Mary. She had needed her husband's permission for everything, even for getting her hair cut. 'This was constant, and she lived a life where she walked on eggshells.' This abuse, he said, had given Mary symptoms of post traumatic stress disorder, simply because 'she didn't know what was going to happen next.' Furthermore, a psychologist testified as part of Mary's defence, saying that her symptoms were those of clinical depression and PTSD.

During her time on the stand, Mary also claimed that Matthew had forced her to watch pornography with him, and that he had bought her several 'slutty' costumes for sex, which she normally would never have worn, but for fear of her husband. If she refused, Matthew wouldn't hesitate to get physical, hitting her or even using his belt to whip her. Mary famously produced a wig and a pair of white high heels in the witness box during her cross-examination to show the court evidence of Matthew's other side.

Mary stated that she was never happy watching pornography, dressing up in sexy outfits or performing the sex acts that Matthew wanted. She went along with his ideas, however, because she didn't dare face his reaction if she didn't. 'I'd just do anything to help him stay happy.' Throughout these revelations, Mary was visibly embarrassed and uncomfortable. Clearly she would have preferred that none of them had ever come to light; but Mary felt it necessary to brave what her neighbors, and the nation, might think in order to clear her name and justify her actions.

Mary's family had been quick to corroborate her side of the story. Her father, Clark Freeman, had spoken out through Good Morning America and detailed the 'physical, mental, verbal' abuse that his daughter had suffered. Other friends came forward during the court case, and gave similar verdicts on their relationship. A friend of Mary's,

Rudie Thomsen, said that '[o]ne Sunday, Mary came into the church and I looked at her and she had a black eye.' Similarly, Mary's friend Amy Redmon agreed that Matthew had been controlling: '[h]e was an authority figure, and he made the decisions basically. It was obvious.'

Conversely, Matthew's family denied that their son had been anything like Mary had depicted in her defence testimony. Matthew's father, Charles Daniel Winkler, said that his son was a kind, gentle man, who could have done nothing to justify what the defence was claiming. Diane spoke several times during the trial, lashing out at Mary: 'You've never told your girls you're sorry! Don't you think you at least owe them that?'

The dramatic story of a supposedly kindly, gentle church minister having such a sordid, cruel and abusive hidden life gripped America. The case was covered extensively on all major networks, discussed on late night panel shows

The Jury's Verdict

While the prosecutors had tried to convince the jury to convict her on a charge of first degree murder, they were unsuccessful. The jury came to their verdict by April, that year. It took them eight hours to deliberate their way to the decision; this mirrored the response of the nation, which was similarly undecided on just what punishment Mary really deserved.

Mary was found guilty of voluntary manslaughter, a charge which carries a far more lenient sentence than murder. While murderers can receive full life sentences, and in certain states receive the death penalty, the maximum sentence for voluntary manslaughter is only 6 years.

Mary showed little emotion at the verdict, but did embrace each of her relatives afterwards. In a show of support, her family had been sat in the row behind her, and all linked arms with one another to demonstrate their solidarity. Afterwards, she was taken back into custody to await sentencing.

Mary's attorney stated afterwards that Mary's testimony had been central in securing the more lenient sentence. 'I think Mary's testimony was integral in this decision. They had to hear it from Mary', Farese told the press. 'They judged her credibility and they saw that she had an abusive relationship and they made their judgment based upon that.'

For Mary, the most important implication of the verdict was that she could finally begin to think of being reunited with her children. Speaking on her behalf after the trial, Farese continued: 'We would like to do so many things to open up communication between Mary and the paternal grandparents and to get the children out of this cycle of constant upheaval over this terrible tragic event.' But the question of how long she would be in prison remained.

Mary's sentencing was scheduled for May 18th, at which point both Mary and the prosecution would have a final chance to address the court before the judge decided on the final jail term. However, the situation looked positive for Mary. Not only would the five months that she had been imprisoned awaiting trial be taken into consideration, but the judge had indicated that alternatives to incarceration would be on the table. Perhaps Mary could avoid jail time altogether.

Sentencing: The Trial at an End

Due to a scheduling error, the hearing took place around three weeks late, on June 8th.

Mary took to the stand one last time to plead for mercy. She read aloud from a prepared statement, telling Matthew's family of her sorrow and remorse for her actions. She was 'so sorry that this had happened', and would 'always miss and love' her husband. 'I ask for mercy and understanding, but I know whatever decision you reach today will be right ... I ask you to please let me go home today and be with my children.' Tabitha Freeman- Mary's sister- had also pleaded for leniency, in particular to let Mary be reunited with her children. She went as far as calling Mary 'the best example of a good person I can think of'.

Members of Matthew's family, too, took to the stand to plead their case for the prosecution. Charles and his wife were clearly hurt and in disbelief at Mary's actions both in murdering their son, and believed that Mary had purposefully smeared his name at trial. 'The monster that you have painted for the world to see? I don't think that monster existed,' Diane Winkler had said.

After speaking their pieces, all that Mary, her family, and Matthew's parents could do was wait until the judge's decision. The trial- as well as the very public 'trial' that Mary had been through in the media- was finally at an end.

The defence had requested that Mary be granted full probation, or judicial diversion, both outcomes which would have meant that Mary would spent no further time in prison, and even that her record would be cleared of wrongdoing altogether. This request was denied.

After recess, Mary was told that she would spend 3 years in prison for her crime. But Circuit Judge J. Weber McCraw reduced that amount to just 210 days total in prison before she would be allowed to leave on probation. She also had that sentence reduced further, due to the fact that she had spent five months incarcerated waiting for trial.

Moreover, that time would be spent not in jail, but in a mental health centre in Tennessee. There, she would receive treatment for both her depression and post traumatic stress disorder. After such a long ordeal, with the prosecution fighting to either put Mary on death row or to imprison her indefinitely, it seemed that she had gotten off with hardly a slap on the wrist.

Steve Farese branded the sentence 'a victory': '[s]he could be in prison for life, and that's what everybody thought she was headed for to begin with.' Her other attorney, Leslie Ballin, said '[s]he'll be able to get out and fight the battle she wants to, and that is to get her children back.' Mary could finally think about the future again.

But certain signs indicated that it would not be as easy to reconcile with her children and family as she might hope. Matthew's family left the courtroom without making a comment to the press, as did the prosecution, clearly disappointed in the verdict. They gave no indication that they would be happy to open dialogue about Mary's daughters- not with the woman whom they believed to have murdered their son in cold blood.

The aftermath of Mary's release

Mary was released on August 14th, 2007. She had only been sentenced the previous June.

Upon her release, her lawyer informed the press that Mary would not be speaking with them, to maintain her privacy. During her time in the mental health facility, Mary could finally begin her attempt to win full custody of her three daughters, and she was still fighting this case at the time of her release. She had not seen her children, apart from Patricia's brief testimony as part of the case, for over a year. Throughout the case, and after Mary's release, her children were staying with Matthew's family.

Moreover, she was still fighting a $2 million dollar civil lawsuit filed by Matthew's parents. They also took legal measures, which, if successful, would have meant that the custody of Mary's children remained with them.

After her release, Mary seemed happier to her family and friends. From an outside perspective, it could be easy to claim that this was just as much due to her happiness at avoiding a jail sentence as it was to her being rid of an abuser. She was in fact living with friends at first after her release, and went back to work at a dry cleaners in McMinnville, Tenn., 200 miles from Selmer.

In the same interview as was mentioned before, Mary's sisters agreed that she had changed entirely. After years of shyness, Mary seeming unable or unwilling to show love to them for fear of her husband's violence, she seemed to finally be able to open up. 'Now it's back to the old Mary [who] loves us and doesn't care to come and hug us and gives us a kiss on the cheek.'

Since then, Mary lived in McMinnville. She has moved between jobs, working at the dry cleaners, before starting work at a nursery. She briefly dated the brother of one of her most vocal supporters, Paul Pillow; afterwards, she moved in with Wayne Cantrell, a preacher living in Smithville nearby.

Mary regained custody of her three children in 2008, but by 2010, received the news that she had multiple sclerosis. Her diagnosis came at the worst time, as she was settling down in her new life; she had not long started medical school with the desire to become a nurse, and had to quit since the work would be too demanding. She hasn't returned to work since.

One comfort for Mary was that Matthew's parents seemed close to being able to forgive her. After her diagnosis, they gave Mary some time off from parenting by taking care of the children for a weekend, which soon turned into several months. Daniel Winkler has preached several times since the events on the topic of forgiveness, although when asked by local press why he chose the topic, he has refused to answer, presumably preferring to keep those details private.

Mary, too, preferred to put the past behind her. In an interview with WAFF 48, the NBC affiliate in Huntsville AL., she stated how she would prefer to stay out of the limelight, particularly for the sake of her girls. 'Whatever reason people have any problem with me, that's fine. Everybody's entitled to their opinion, but these girls are treated for who they are, not because of what their mother's done ... They're three very fine young ladies'.

Concluding Thoughts

Some members of the public reacted with disgust at the abnormally short sentence that Mary was given, and questioned whether a husband would have been given the same leniency as Mary was. Men's rights activist Glenn Sacks publicly questioned whether a